The Lorette Wilmot Library
Nazareth College of Rochester

TOTAL QUALITY ACCOUNTING

TOTAL QUALITY ACCOUNTING

MICHAEL D. WOODS, CPA

JOHN WILEY & SONS, INC.

New York • Chichester • Brisbane • Toronto • Singapore

This publication is designed to provide accurate and
authoritative information in regard to the subject
matter covered. It is sold with the understanding that
the publisher is not engaged in rendering legal, accounting,
or other professional services. If legal advice or other
expert assistance is required, the services of a competent
professional person should be sought.

Library of Congress Cataloging-in-Publication Data:
Woods, Michael D., 1947–
　　Total quality accounting / Michael D. Woods.
　　　　p.　　cm.
　　Includes index.
　　ISBN 0-471-31185-5
　　1. Cost accounting.　2. Total quality management.　I. Title.
　　HF5686.C8W74　1994
　　657'.068'5—dc20
　　　　　　　　　　　　　　　　　　　　　　　94-334
　　　　　　　　　　　　　　　　　　　　　　　CIP

Printed in the United States of America

10 9 8 7 6 5 4 3 2

CONTENTS

PREFACE

Total quality accounting is a new approach to cost accounting. It uses the methods of the total quality management movement to fit accounting products to managers' needs. Total quality management or TQM is the name given to these practices, which were advocated by W. Edwards Deming, Joseph Juran, Philip Crosby, and others in 1984. But the roots of TQM lie with statistical quality control techniques developed in the 1920s. Statistical quality control took off during the 1940s when inexperienced workers were rapidly assimilated into the war effort; these workers needed to be trained and made productive quickly and their products had to be dependable. American authorities took these quality control techniques with them to Japan to aid in post-war reconstruction. In Japan the approach was further developed to include employee participation in work design. A focus on customers led to defining *quality* as "fitness for use." "Quality" is the defining framework of total quality management. It is probably best expressed in Deming's 14 points, although not all practitioners would agree with each of them exactly as Deming wrote them.

From this basis, the Japanese went on to develop *quality circles* and *just-in-time* or *Kanban* inventory control techniques using TQM principles. They established a world competitive position that threatened many American industries, forcing a radical response. That response has been to re-apply those principles exported to Japan in the 1940s and to accept those Japanese developments that are applicable to the U.S. situation, as well as making further progress ourselves.

The total quality movement has now taken hold in American industry. It is past the "fad-and-fashion" stage, and has become a well-established norm. It has given us competitive products at competitive prices throughout the manufacturing sector and it is moving into the service sector as well.

I was fortunate to be part of an early and highly successful total quality management implementation beginning in 1984. As we all learned new ways of doing things, it was clear that the design engineers and manufacturing engineers recognized the concepts involved. Line workers took to the total quality approach enthusiastically after they saw its effectiveness.

But employing total quality management to the staff was second priority, and no one seemed to know how to do it. The accounting function was especially difficult. When the concepts were first introduced to our management group I argued that they should also be applied to our cost accounting procedures and outputs. The manufacturing and engineering department head said,

"No! That's just what we won't do!" He thought I meant to track the costs of the total quality implementation, never imagining anyone would want total quality accounting. That kind of suspicion seems endemic in traditional industrial companies, where the designers don't trust sales or accounting, the manufacturers don't trust designers or accounting, and sales doesn't trust manufacturing or accounting. Accounting departments, since no one else likes them, report the truth according to their own interpretations, regardless of whether these truths are useful in others' daily work.

As line managers awaken to total quality practices, they refuse to accept the accounting products they have been given. Because accounting's internal customers demand better information, accounting departments are learning to break down barriers and join the company team. One result is that accounting departments have been discovering new ways to view and to report cost behavior. (We've actually been rediscovering the basic principles of cost accounting and re-applying them to the new manufacturing situation.) After a theoretical discussion lasting, off and on, since the 1950s, direct costing principles are now guiding decisions. Activity-based costing has been developed to improve the relevance of cost assignment among organizational segments, particularly when they use one another's products or share resources. Attention is also being paid to non-dollar measures and to methods of estimating the value of qualitative improvements in products and processes.

When participating in the total quality management implementation, I hoped these TQM techniques would someday become accepted practices in the tool kit of American industrial companies, and spread beyond purely industrial companies to service and financial service companies. And they have spread, though not yet as far as I hoped. The slow spread of Total Quality concepts to services, especially to accounting, troubles me because I have sympathies on both sides. I am an accountant myself, but one with an interest in technical subjects, having taught aerodynamics at the Navy's Flight Instructor Training Program. But I can understand the opposite point of view since I have engineers on both sides of the family. It seems a shame that two groups I admire and who have much in common through their ready understanding of analytical methods are at odds in so many organizations.

I had hoped to see line workers and accountants striving together to promote effectiveness and efficiency in our organizations. But despite fundamental changes in the way we manage, it seems that the line workers and staff accountants are still talking past one another. We now have a common purpose, which is certainly an improvement over the old ways, but we still appear to speak different languages and base our contributions on different assumptions. It's as though we are from different countries, but are learning to live together. A lack of guidance on how to integrate total quality practices with cost accounting is a handicap in our efforts to understand one another and to work together.

In 1984 I expected no explicit guidance for line and accounting workers who were creating total quality accounting in a total quality organization but 10 years later I had hoped there would be more material addressing accounting issues. There still isn't much that speaks directly to the problem, so I have set out to provide what I can from personal experience, discussion with others, and study as a starting point for both line managers and accountants. The purpose of this book is to bring line managers and accountants together in using the total quality process to create total quality accounting. It is organized in three parts:

Part 1. *Total Quality Management*—where it came from, what it involves, and how it's done.

Part 2. *Cost Accounting*—its first principles, how they can be applied, how they have been applied in the past, and what's new.

Part 3. *Total Quality Accounting*—how to become a total quality accounting department in a total quality company, the importance of pleasing the internal customer, and what practices can be used to help do so.

A brief closing section considers new directions in industry and how accountants can contribute to the next set of competitive challenges.

This book is both for line managers and for accountants. It is for line managers who want to further the total quality cause by extending it to their accounting department. And it is for accountants who want to know more about total quality concepts and practices but are afraid to ask or don't easily follow all the industrial engineering and statistical language in most books. It is also for accountants who observe total quality methodology taking hold in their companies and want to be part of it, but don't know where to begin or how to do it.

I have tried to avoid mathematical details, partly because TQM implementations require trained statisticians anyway. Readers must only recognize the need for applications. The main reason for avoiding mathematical details, though, is that rigorous statistical techniques are not generally applicable to the most urgent accounting changes we need to make. Although more efficient accounting processes reduce overall organizational costs, even the reduced costs are wasted money if the products are not what the accounting customer needs. And those needs are best determined by more subjective means, chiefly by inquiry. Some situations require rigorous inquiry in accordance with market research principles. Another way to get user opinion is to include those users on improvement teams.

Not all readers will need to read all parts of the book. Cost accountants facing the unfamiliar terrain of total quality implementation should read the first part. Total quality workers who want to see into the mysteries of accounting should read the second part. Both groups should read the third part, which builds upon and integrates the first two. And general managers who are beginning total quality efforts and who want to include them in their accounting function should read all three parts.

I offer this book to help us bring our skills together in a new alliance leading to better products for our customers. I hope these insights and experiences will be as interesting and useful to others as they have been to me and that the result will be the elimination of barriers to communication and cooperation within your company.

PART I

INTRODUCTION TO TOTAL QUALITY MANAGEMENT

In order to fully understand total quality accounting, the reader should have a basic knowledge of the total quality management movement. Part 1 of this text is designed for those of you who are new to total quality management. We will briefly discuss the basic concepts and techniques of TQM before we move on to how those techniques can be implemented to create a total quality accounting strategy.

1

WHAT IS TOTAL QUALITY MANAGEMENT?

BRIEF HISTORY OF TQM

The total quality management (TQM) movement can be traced to three "gurus" who achieved renown in the 1970s and 1980s. They are Philip Crosby, W. Edwards Deming, and Joseph Juran—all Americans.

Among these early TQM leaders, Philip Crosby offered more of a practical, step-by-step model. This came naturally to him since his industrial career had been in quality control functions. Joseph M. Juran was a statistician who offered practical applications of statistical theory with some added management approaches. His strength was with decisions based on analysis of data. W. Edwards Deming is a theoretical statistician who, in applying his knowledge to production in WWII, discovered management principles that grew into total quality management.

Deming's 14 Points

In his nineties, Deming was still giving seminars and writing on quality in industry. (Regrettably, he passed away late last year.) His work stresses a number of key items:

1. Commitment.
2. Statistical process control rather than inspection (he's a statistician by training).
3. Cooperation among employees and departments within an organization.
4. Cooperation with suppliers.
5. Meeting customer requirements.

Deming has expressed these items in 14 key points. These points are used in some form in every TQM implementation, but he doesn't insist on them as if they were written in stone. Deming was always learning and modified his points if given sufficient reason. As they stand, they are:

1. Create constancy of purpose for improvement of product and service.
2. Adopt the new philosophy.
3. Cease dependence on mass inspection.
4. End the practice of awarding business on price tag alone.
5. Improve constantly and forever the system of production and service.
6. Institute training.
7. Institute leadership.
8. Drive out fear.
9. Break down barriers between staff areas.
10. Eliminate slogans, exhortation, and targets for the workforce.
11. Eliminate numerical quotas.
12. Remove barriers to pride of workmanship.
13. Institute a vigorous program of education and retraining.
14. Take action to accomplish the transformation.

Deming gives credit for much of his success to Walter A. Shewhart, a statistician at Bell Telephone Laboratories in New York with whom Deming studied, and his work in the 1920s and 1930s. Shewhart developed practical applications of statistics in industrial quality control, leading to accepted methods of statistical quality control that have not changed their basis even today.

Development of these TQM principles continued in Japan after WWII when the United States wanted to help rebuild Japanese industry. The Japanese were anxious to learn how such fine war materials could be made in such quantity and Deming, among others, went to Japan to teach American war production techniques. He was such a success there that today the Japanese national prize for industrial excellence is called the Deming Prize.

Crosby's Quality Improvement Program

Among the quality management leaders mentioned earlier was Philip B. Crosby. Crosby has worked primarily in the United States, unlike Deming, who worked for a long time in post-war reconstruction Japan.

Crosby's work is different from Deming's in other ways too. He offers a practical program of defined steps to achieve a successful quality improvement program, emphasizing application as well as education and philosophy. But his work is similar to Deming's in many ways as well. It emphasizes the need for consistency and constancy of purpose. It requires a long-term commitment, since it will take a long time to realize the full benefits of the program. And it requires enlisting the cooperation of the workforce and suppliers—not manipulating them, but honestly changing the company approach to business and allowing them to join the effort in a fully informed, real way.

Just as every total quality management implementation takes much of its attitudinal (cognitive and effective to educators) aspect from Deming, it takes much of its practical aspect (cognitive and psychomotor to educators) from Crosby. Not every implementation uses every part of the program, but all use some of them or something like them. Philip Crosby, in the seminal book *Quality Is Free*, states that he has never seen a failure when all his steps are used in the thorough way he advocates.

You will certainly encounter Crosby's principles, or variations of them in your TQM effort. You should be acquainted with Philip Crosby's program in order to participate in the program your own company or department implements. If you share responsibility for designing the program, you must know these steps in order to develop an effective plan. Here are the steps of Crosby's program:

1. Management commitment.
2. Quality improvement team.
3. Quality measurement.
4. Cost of quality evaluation.
5. Quality awareness.
6. Corrective action.
7. Establish an ad hoc committee for the zero defects program.
8. Supervisor training.
9. Zero defects day.
10. Goal setting.
11. Error-cause removal.
12. Recognition.
13. Quality Councils.
14. Do it over again.

When the development of total quality management in Japan virtually closed down the American electronics and shipbuilding industries (though the Japanese have since lost ground in these areas) and seriously threatened the automobile industry, we began to take notice. After our usual approaches didn't work, we began to copy and adapt some of the Japanese practices. We copied practices they had originally copied from us!

Such companies as Texas Instruments and Hewlett Packard, in electronics, and Ford, in automobiles, using TQM techniques, gave us the microcomputer and the highly successful Taurus. They retain solid competitive position with these products because of their practice of total quality management. They possess no magic. Anyone can do the same, but it takes commitment from top management, resources, and time to make such a dramatic change in our old ways of doing business. We can no longer force change from "experts" on intelligent workers; we will lose too much potential talent.

BASIC PRINCIPLES OF TQM

There are many technical aspects to total quality management, including sophisticated mathematical techniques, but the most basic principles are just that—basic. By now, most of us have heard of them or read of them in the popular business press. Each new, fast-growing business can point to its dedication to these principles, but few can demonstrate the use of the specific practices that are part of the "real and total" total quality management. That is one reason why so many businesses start with a flurry of success, but then level off or decline. They do not establish a mechanism for constant improvement, and competitors move ahead of them in the marketplace. They fall behind in design, in the product itself, in delivery, or in all three areas.

But total quality management can provide means of staying ahead in the competitive race, as our international competitors and an ever-larger number of American companies are demonstrating. The applied basic principles of total quality management create an organization that is:

1. Customer focused;
2. Data driven; and
3. Participatory.

What does each of these principles mean in practice?

Customer Focused

Too often we spend our time taking care of our own organization and our own duties rather than taking care of the customer. It seems to be a universal tendency for every organization to deteriorate into a bureaucracy, at least in its administrative and service arms. Recently I was in the famous customer-focused store, WalMart. The bigwigs had decided to offer customers 24-hour service—a good idea when I needed more paint at 7 AM. But there was only one lane open, the clerk stopped several minutes for a price check, the supervisor at an adjoining station kept writing on some forms rather than opening another line for the four of us who were waiting (despite WalMart's promise about opening another line for three), and when the clerk returned, she got into a conversation with another clerk about some stocking issue. The point is not that WalMart has problems, but that even the best customer-focused organizations have trouble staying on track. The natural tendency is to get our own paperwork in order rather than to accomplish the ultimate purpose of the organization.

Total quality management keeps a customer focus by constantly stressing customer's needs. It tells us that we must keep in touch with our customers, both the end-users of our company's products and those within the company who use the output of our own process. The question, of course, is how we do this. Traditionally, it is the marketing department's job to find out what the customer wants, engineering's job to design it, planning's job to establish the production process, manufacturing's job to make it, and shipping's job to get it out. Each function throws its specifications over the wall to the next. One result is that the item the customer really wanted is sometimes very different from what is finally brought to market. Long development cycles can result as each function waits for the preceding one in the chain to finish its work before it begins its own effort in moving the original idea toward the marketplace.

TQM can cure such conditions as members from all levels of the organization participate in getting close to the customer. One means is through customer visits. Groups of workers actually visit customers and see the company's products in use. They can ask users about the products, how well they work, and what might improve them. And what an impression it makes on the customers when a supplier and its workers care this much!

The second way of getting close to the customer applies within the organization and relates to the participatory nature of TQM. Employee participation in product and work design includes being part of *quality circles* and *action teams*, where they join with members of downstream departments and processes to discuss how their work can be performed better and their products can be made more usable in the hands of the next processing step. In this way, each worker has regular contact with internal customers of "his" processes and learns what the customer needs.

Data Driven

Being data driven is an answer to Deming's question "How do you know?" For example, when someone says "My adding machine doesn't work," we often begin guessing what might be wrong, and suggesting what the user might try to get it going. Or some of the staff suggest calling a repairman or getting a new machine. To find a sure way to effect repair, though, a more disciplined, systematic approach is needed. We can begin by learning how the machine is supposed to work, then observing its behavior, and finally performing tests to determine the real fault. Then we can fix it. Or, as is sometimes the case, we will discover that training was lacking; the machine was OK but we didn't know about all its features and caused the apparent problem ourselves.

The adding machine example is not a perfect one because it requires repairmen. It is a cheap operation. But an industrial process is not cheap and each is unique. There are no repairmen. We who do the work are the real experts. The example does, however, teach us that we must know what's really wrong before we can fix it. And that requires knowledge.

There is no substitute for data in answering a question about product or service quality. Guesses, suppositions, and anecdotes will not do. The necessary data consist of two parts: data on what the customer needs and wants, and data on how the product or service is actually delivered and performs in use.

Participatory

Total quality management enlists the talents of each member of the organization to improve the quality of service. The previous section mentioned *quality circles* and *action teams*. These are the mechanisms through which an organization can enlist the creative energy of each willing worker. We must ensure that the employees' efforts are directed toward the organization's reason for being—services and products. Once workers know what their work is for (customer focus) and how it actually comes out in practice (data driven), they can apply their talents to improving their products by improving their work processes. Processes can be improved from original product concepts through design, production, and delivery. And it can be done for internal products as well as for ultimate products.

Mechanisms for process improvement include permanent councils in each work section, with representatives of related sections both downstream and upstream in the overall process, and temporary teams for specific problems. The councils are called by various names: quality circles, quality management boards, or process groups, among others. The teams also have a variety of names, such as process action teams, process improvement teams, or simply action teams.

Quality circles need about an hour or so a week with a planned agenda of process-related items to review. They may resolve a problem, appoint a team to look into it further, pass it to a circle nearer to the likely source, or decide it does not warrant further attention.

If the quality circle decides on more investigation, it will often appoint an action team whose charter is to investigate further, gathering data and proposing action to improve the production process. But the action team's charter is limited to the problem it is assigned. If it discovers other opportunities, the team must refer them to the chartering circle for consideration. An action team dissolves when its particular problem is resolved. New teams are constituted for new problems. Action teams include members of the quality circle that charters them, and usually members of related work sections. Engineering, legal, or other outside experts may also be appointed if it seems advisable. By using quality circles and action teams, companies can enlist the creative energies of their employees. When these energies are directed to the right ends through customer-focused contacts and through evaluation based on data, a company's employees can become its competitive edge.

But employees are smart; they'll spot a phony. So be prepared to invest the necessary resources of outside assistance and time during the work day. Hundreds of companies here and overseas have found it well worth the cost.

Shewhart Cycle of Continuous Improvement

One of the pioneers of statistical process control and the management methods that developed from its application was Walter A. Shewhart. The Shewhart cycle is sometimes called the PDCA cycle after its steps: *Plan, Do, Check, Act*. Another name for this cycle is the Deming cycle after W. Edwards Deming, who advocates its use. However, Deming himself identifies it as the *Shewhart Cycle* in deference to his old teacher, from whom he learned it.

The Shewhart cycle is one of continuous improvement because new problems and opportunities are constantly sought for its application and because the same opportunities are constantly revisited for further improvement. The four steps must be kept in balance or efforts will be less than optimum. If it's all planning and no doing, the plans were a waste of time. If it's all unplanned doing, there is no purpose and no efficiency in the doing. If there's no checking, we have no idea whether the plans and execution had the desired effect, or any effect at all. And if there's no action based on the checking, we have accepted the actual results even if they differ from those we wanted. So we plan as much as we can do, do as much as we can check, and check as much as we can act upon.

Since the Shewhart Cycle is one of continuous improvement, we don't stop after acting on our checking. We begin again with planning our next doing, and so on, so that process improvement and product improvement go on without end. We're always getting better. The improvements envisioned are usually incremental process improvements, making the production and service processes better by little bits. But the cycle can also be applied to major redesign projects and to new businesses.

TQM TRAINING

Total quality management is no longer new to many companies. Some have practiced it for eight years or more, but it is new to most of industry. It was once new to its current practitioners, too, and their experience bears out the statements of the quality movement leaders: it takes initial and recurrent training in the use of TQM tools for any effort to be successful.

There is much that could be said about training for a TQM implementation and its later, sustained effort: What subjects? Who should do it? What methods are best? How much math? These subjects are discussed in later chapters; they are the content of total quality management.

To summarize, the process of total quality management training begins with awareness at the top and is spread simultaneously down the organization and into the details of applying specific TQM tools. In this way, the whole organization becomes aware of what can be done and begins to improve its processes as its members learn to use new techniques and relationships with confidence.

While total quality management training will certainly be emphasized during initial implementation, it cannot be allowed to permanently supplant training and education in production skills, inventory management, finance, or whatever each employee's primary contribution to the company may be. Indeed, such job skill training is itself a quality and process improvement step and may properly be a recommendation of a process team or quality circle when it addresses an improvement opportunity. As total quality management demands training in TQM techniques, it is also likely to increase the amount of job training in other skills.

CULTURAL DIFFERENCES BETWEEN JAPAN AND THE UNITED STATES—CAN WE APPLY TQM HERE?

As we've already discussed, total quality management in the United States began with statistical quality control methods that were developed from the early 1900s through WWII. When WWII ended, the Japanese expressed admiration for the quantity and quality of American armaments. Saburo Sakai, Japan's leading fighter pilot in that war, marveled at the fit and finish of American airplanes. And those planes, so beautifully assembled, were produced at the previously unbelievable rate of thousands each month. The methods that made that possible were assiduously copied by the Japanese in their post-war process design techniques, where each item that rolled off the line was identical to the one before.

Variation in the American war production effort was eliminated through rapid, consistent training of new workers; there wasn't time and there weren't enough older craftsmen for "following Joe around" to work as a training technique. Variation was also eliminated through statistical process control. Thus, when a product began to be made right, it stayed right for the rest of its run.

The Japanese contributed some aspects of their own culture, though. Their culture is more cooperative than competitive, at least within each company and *keiretsu* (group of cooperating companies). The quality circles that they developed from their cooperative approach to making a uniform product, coupled with the customer focus that resulted from the cooperation within *keiretsu*, led to the invention of additional TQM techniques. Just in time or JIT is the most well-known example.

When the uniformity and customer focus of Japanese production began to present a competitive challenge in the U.S. home market, we took up the TQM banner. There have been some notable successes in the United States, as well as some failures.

Why have some U.S. efforts proved disappointing or even been abandoned? One reason commonly cited is a basic difference in culture. It is thought that a uniform cultural background, especially a compliant, cooperative one, is more conducive to cooperative effort. Americans can cooperate, but there are differences in the approaches that work in our two countries. The U.S. culture produced victorious forces partly by using early, basic TQM techniques. They are an American invention, not a Japanese one. Also, our military forces were victorious because the whole country was behind them. That's the difference between successful and unsuccessful TQM implementations—constancy and unity of purpose. That was the difference between the results of WWII and Desert Storm (the "Mother of all Battles" lasted only four days), on one hand, and Vietnam on the other. In our successful military expeditions we had common agreement among citizens, soldiers, and Congress about what was to be done and why. Citizens sent packages to soldiers and welcomed them home. In Vietnam, no one seemed in agreement and the soldiers were treated badly by many of the citizens and even by some members of the Congress whose resolutions made their commitment to battle possible under our laws.

So it's possible to obtain success in American TQM implementations. It just takes a more comprehensive approach to elicit full cooperation from all workers. The resulting total quality solutions are likely to be better, though, because the American "tossed salad" of cultures offers more possible approaches to a problem than a uniform culture might.

What are some of the differences that a typical American company will have to consider? We differ from the Japanese and even among ourselves in many ways. One difference is the strength and independence of our unions. In Japan, unions are "sweetheart unions" by American standards. Here they are independent of the company, though in a sense, of course, dependent on its existence. TQM can't succeed without union cooperation (where there are unions, of course). The company's and union members' interdependence is a key to success. The interests of the managers, stockholders, and union members are similar in that all depend on customer satisfaction and market acceptance of the ultimate product to attain their goals. Of course the union may see TQM as a threat to the members if it looks like the "fad of the year," designed to get more work out of the members and possibly even to cost some of them their jobs. But if the union is brought in early and if the union members see TQM as a means to continued employment and a bigger pie to share, cooperation can be achieved. The trust that comes from early involvement is the essential ingredient for TQM success in the union environment.

Another difference between U.S. and Japanese business is not commonly recognized. Although we think of lifetime employment in Japan, that is the case only in the few large companies whose names we recognize. Living in the country for two years (one off the military base) as a military member hardly makes me an expert, but I was struck by the many industrial plants that looked slapped together, even in the 1980s, and whose names I didn't recognize. The large number of small establishments was also striking. A little investigation showed that most Japanese work in small businesses, many of which are suppliers to larger ones, or suppliers to suppliers, and many of which are family craft shops or retail stores dealing with consumers. None of these offer lifetime security and most offer no fringe benefits. The small businesses that are forced by their customers to supply materials with statistical evidence of quality control or to supply materials on a just-in-time basis get some exposure to total quality management, but most of Japan seemed less susceptible to TQM implementation than most of the United States.

The conclusion to be drawn is that the United States is culturally suited to total quality management, but it requires different techniques to elicit worker commitment. American workers are less blindly obedient, but more enthusiastic when they see reasons to join the effort. And therein lies the uniquely American opportunity to surpass the Japanese (and many other international competitors as well).

2

"QUALITY" IS KEY IN TQM

USING TQM TO IMPROVE EMPLOYEE EFFECTIVENESS AND COMMUNICATIONS

As total quality management training is conducted throughout the hierarchy of any organization, each level needs to act promptly on its new knowledge before these new skills grow stale and enthusiasm wanes. There are at least three reasons for this: First, action will give concrete shape to the knowledge gained, cementing it in the minds of the workers and managers. Second, action will provide the psychomotor dimension that academics define as a primary dimension of learning. (That is, our workers and managers will learn to do as well as learning to know.) Third, the goal of every organization is to produce a defined product or service. It's only by actually employing TQM techniques that the principles are translated into *quality* in those products and services. Quality is key to all TQM efforts. Quality can be achieved through many different techniques. Let's start with a discussion of TQM techniques for improving employee communications.

Quality Circles

The chance to act on new knowledge occurs in quality circles, where free discussion of work-related and process-related methods, tools, and procedures can yield new and better ways of conducting the company's business. The name *quality circle* comes from Japan, where consensus in work design is more a part of the cooperative culture than in the competitive work culture found here. In the United States, other terms are more common, such as quality management boards, quality councils, or quality improvement groups. Quality circles are permanent parts of a total quality management structure within an organization.

Quality circles meet on a regular basis to discuss improvement opportunities in work processes. Quality circles should include supervisors and members from all parts of the organization; even personnel who are upstream or downstream from the core membership's area, including customers and suppliers. In this way, suppliers and customers can be represented when discussing product and process quality issues.

These quality circles exist at every organizational level, as each worker, from president to janitor, meets periodically to discuss task-related problems and opportunities with peers and a few representatives of other work sections. An executive quality circle, for example, would consist of the top management group, but should include a few middle managers to provide a "reality check." A janitorial quality circle could include a plant or industrial engineer and a line worker or two to provide assurance that all needs are met as the janitorial process becomes more efficient and effective.

Action Teams

Like quality circles, *action teams* have different names in different organizations. They may be called process action teams, process improvement teams, or quality improvement teams, but their functions are the same whatever they are called. Quality circles are permanent structures with regular meetings for raising and resolving issues that either inhibit quality production or could add to the quality of the members' processes and products. Sometimes the quality circle finds that it is unable to reach a conclusion because it has too little information. In such cases, an action team may be formed to look into the matter. An action team has a specific charter from the sponsoring QC, including objective, time permitted, team membership, and other resources available.

There are a few characteristics of these teams that the new TQM student might not expect to find. First, they work within the normal management structure. They have a manager of appropriate seniority assigned as chairman so that their suggestions will receive proper consideration and so that resources can be commanded where necessary. Second, they report to their chartering QC first but their recommendations must be approved and implemented on the authority of the normal management structure. Third, their resources are sufficient for the job, including financial resources for experimental materials and travel to other sites where possible solutions are in use. While resources are sufficient for the job, they are also scaled to the hoped-for results of the job, so the costs and benefits stay in proportion. TQM is, after all, practical. Fourth, action teams are privileged to go where they need to go in a facility to get the information they need, but they don't have unlimited freedom to wander the company. They must answer clear and specific questions.

If an action team discovers other matters, they must have their charter expanded or refer the matter to the chartering QC for another team to be constituted for the new issue. The decision as to whether to expand the charter, constitute another team, or pass the matter to a more directly involved QC rests with the chartering circle. The team's powers are limited to using its resources to answer the questions posed for it.

With action teams, as throughout total quality management, the keys are preparation, training, top level commitment, and adequate resources of time, personnel, and materials.

Vision Statements

A *vision statement* that sets forth a company's outlook and its values can condition the responses and behavior of every member of an organization. But to do so, it must be believed and accepted by all, or at least a very large portion of the organization's members. Only direction and persistence from the top can ensure the credibility that will bring about such acceptance. And full participation by representative members of various levels of the organization can aid in acceptance by workers and supervisors as they become part of the TQM effort.

Consequently, a vision statement might be best crafted by a committee of the executive quality circle. I do not suggest an action team, though some companies might want to use one, because the vision statement is not a concrete productivity or quality problem; but it is a task that could be stated as a problem if the action team mechanics were desired. The committee could include some middle managers, some supervisors, and some senior workers who know the organization well. The executive quality circle will, of course, give the committee guidance in stating the goal of the committee and will provide resources of company time, staff and professional assistance, and reference materials.

Vision statements may include several brief sentences describing the organization's values. Each usually begins, "We are . . . ," "We value . . . ," "We seek opportunities to . . . ," or similar wording.

Some examples are:

"We are an organization of individuals with varied roles at work, in the community, and at home, each of whom has chosen to commit the work portion of his or her time and effort to the success of X Corporation in business, in its community, and in society at large."

"We value each member's contribution and seek ways to assist one another in improving our contributions to the productive enterprise of X Corporation while respecting the dignity and right to differing opinions among ourselves."

Typically, three to six such sentences are enough for any vision statement. Too few don't give enough direction and too many can't be kept in mind, so they are not acted on consistently. Be comprehensive but concise when drafting your vision statement.

Codes of Conduct

To support the vision statement, more specific guidance is usually required in the form of a *code of conduct*. As with the vision statement, a committee of the executive quality circle is a good way to develop a code, though certainly not the only way. In a union environment, union representation can help ensure acceptance throughout the company. Again, many levels should be represented.

Many of us are familiar with the code of conduct of the United States Armed Forces. It prescribes certain kinds of actions in case of capture by the enemy, such as, "If senior, I will take command" and "I will give only my name, rank, service number, and date of birth." A business code of conduct serves a similar purpose. It tells individuals how to act in certain situations where rules are lacking or when the heat of the moment makes it easy to forget the vision statement.

In total quality management efforts, a code of conduct is useful for demonstrating the organization's commitment to its vision, for guiding employees in daily actions, and for underlining management's desire to bring about the changes implied by the total quality philosophy. If your company is embarking on TQM implementation, a code of conduct may be helpful in bringing success.

Mission Statements

As you will recall, a vision statement is a statement of values; it's a statement of how the company views itself and its character or personality. Codes of conduct help guide a company in the direction of its vision. The *mission statement* is an explication not of what the organization is, but of what it does. For example, on a more personal level, an individual's vision statement might say, "I am a contributor to my family and community. I believe in the sanctity of the home and in the values of the U.S. Constitution. I am politically conservative and Catholic. I value peace, order, and friendship." But an individual's mission statement might say, "I train my children to obey the law and to work in their schools and church. I contribute to my country's economy and earn a living by designing employee benefit plans for medium-sized companies. I provide for the material needs of my family. I participate in professional and church activities." An individual who knows what he does and what's important to him will be more effective at those things as he unconsciously sets priorities that bring about the intended results.

In the same way, a total quality company needs to communicate clearly to its workers, customers, suppliers, and community that it does something—that it has a mission. By stating plainly what the organization's purpose is, those who are willing can follow; they know what they are working for if they are workers or suppliers; they know what to expect if they are customers. Those who read and accept the mission statement can unconsciously set priorities that lead to mission accomplishment—that lead to the organization doing what it intends to do. Side tracks are minimized; all effort can be concentrated on achieving the purposes the company has adopted.

Successful mission statements are prepared within the TQM structure—usually by an action team or committee of the executive quality circle. This way, each member of the organization is integrated into the total quality structure and procedures. Each member can see that these statements were prepared using the same process. Preparation of the statement by the TQM structure and process lends a sense of ownership to each individual.

Individual Most Important Job Statements

Just as a work unit can get caught up in the details of daily work and lose sight of the company mission statement an individual can forget his or her "mission" in the crush of daily tasks. Short-term, personal objectives are easier to keep in mind so that when the pressure of daily events gets to be too much, there's still a guiding statement for reference, something telling the worker what his or her priorities are for the day. The statement that provides this guidance is an *individual mission statement*, but I prefer the name *most important job statement*.

A most important job is the task or objective that, if accomplished, justifies the worker's employment. It is the thing that must be done even if nothing else is. It is the unit that the worker passes along the line to contribute to the company's ultimate product and the company's mission.

Within the most important job statement there may be several distinct tasks, such as sorting supplier invoices, matching invoices to purchase orders and receiving reports, entering invoices into supplier computer files, and designating invoices for payment. All of them are part of the most important job and should be first priority when in conflict with duties that contribute less directly to the company mission. No matter how hectic things get, the employee can refer to the most important job statement and be assured that as long as she's working on that job, she's doing the right thing. She can know that she's an integral part of accomplishing the company mission.

CRITICAL SUCCESS FACTORS—MEASURING QUALITY

Once an organization has defined its character through its vision statements and has stated its purpose through a mission statement, the company is ready to execute its mission. Each component of the organization can focus its effort on its special contribution to the company's reason for being, and each individual, by doing his or her "most important job," can ensure that the aspect of his or her work that contributes most to the company's objectives is top priority.

Individual workers and organizational units, although concentrating on accomplishing their particular missions, will need measures of their success—ways to tell whether they are achieving all that they should. These measures are provided through *critical success factors* defined by each unit and each individual in a total quality management implementation. Critical success factors are those tasks that, if done well, ensure that the mission or most important job is also done well.

Because most missions are related to providing output to a customer, critical success factors will generally be those features of the organizational unit's output that are most valued by the customer. For example, in accounting reports, readability may be a critical success factor. Quality of paper or precision of estimates may not be critical, depending on who is using the reports and for what purpose. In production shops, an aircraft landing gear bearing surface dimension may be a critical success factor, whereas smoothness of outer surfaces may not. In marketing, package design may be a critical success factor, whereas package material may not, again depending on the circumstances. Each product has some critical success factors associated with it. Those factors are features valued by the user of the product, the customer, or those that are necessary for valued features to be perceived and to benefit the customer.

WORKING WITH CUSTOMERS TO ACHIEVE QUALITY

One of the primary goals of total quality management is to "get close to the customer." The customer, after all, is the reason for your work. Anything that benefits the person who uses your output is an added value. Anything that interferes with use or enjoyment of your output is a reduction in value and quality. By getting close to your customers, you can make your products more useful and valuable.

Getting close to the customer involves the aspects of quality we usually think of—those aspects involved with making better chairs, pencils, or whatever. It also involves the question of whether your customer really needs those chairs or pencils at all, in other words, of discovering the customer's real need and meeting it, rather than just altering the product you're currently selling. There are a number of ways to get close to your customers. A personal relationship is what probably comes to mind when the phrase "close to the customer" is first heard. That is certainly a valuable way to let the customer know you care about his needs. It also allows you to hear about shortfalls in service before they become a sufficient irritant to the customer that he takes his business elsewhere.

Besides the informal methods implied by "just getting acquainted," there are formal methods akin to data-gathering. For instance, if the customer will permit it, you can chart customer processes to see how your product is used. Your designers and workers can visit the customer's place of business to see the products in use. You may be permitted to take measurements of the variability of your products going into the customer's processes and of the variability of the customer's products. But what if your customers are too diverse and scattered for direct visits? There are still tools available to gather data on your products' uses and performance—namely, market research. Market research begins with the discovery of a need that can be filled, or even earlier, with a decision to search for needs that can be filled.

Getting close to the customer means getting to know him or her personally, where possible, or through market research methods, where necessary. It means creating expectations that can be fulfilled and not over-promising. It means constant improvement in service and product design so that the products can more exactly fill the customers' needs. It means improving the product all the time, both in features and design.

WORKING WITH SUPPLIERS TO IMPROVE QUALITY

The production process for a particular item or service doesn't start with your own business. The product that ends up in your customer's hands is made of material that came from your suppliers and was sold, assembled, or transformed in other ways by your company. These inputs to your production process are very much a part of the quality of your work and of the product that your customer receives. Although it seems that your suppliers should be responsible for their own products, your customer won't see it that way. You will get or lose business based on your final product. If a supplier causes a problem, you'll take the hit.

The material or service that a supplier gives you isn't the only thing that affects your profitability and your ability to serve your customers. Delivery terms and schedules matter, too, since having too much material on hand can lead to deterioration as well as to moving and storage costs with attendant damage and loss. Having too little leads to costly special orders and work stoppages or work-arounds.

Total quality management offers a way to avoid problems of these kinds. It gives you the means of having the material and services of the type and quality you need in a usable form at the required time and place. The key is contained in Deming's fourth point, "End the practice of awarding business on price tag alone." Instead of bidding and getting material and services from whoever is cheapest each day, form long-lasting relationships with your suppliers.

The supplier is assured of a long-term, loyal customer who will continue to buy and whose needs are therefore worth some investment, and you are assured of a long-term, loyal supplier whose output will conform to your requirements and who will make the necessary investment to give you what you and your customers need.

Of course, awarding business on any basis other than price involves deciding what those other bases should be and what weight should be given to each. Some factors that can be considered are:

- Price
- Delivery
- Lot size
- Quality control methods
- Flexibility
- Payment terms
- Engineering capability
- Range of materials that can be worked
- Skill of workforce
- Commitment to training of workers
- Ancillary services, such as training for our workers
- Proximity
- Reciprocal relationships
- Exclusivity in certain products
- Investment in facilities

One of the main factors that, under the total quality philosophy, should influence sourcing decisions is quality control methods employed by suppliers. Since you are committing yourself to statistical quality control in your own operation, you must evaluate the quality of your incoming material in the same way. Some Japanese companies insist that each lot of incoming material be packed with the statistical process control chart made during its production. In this way, they can see exactly what the lot mean and variation were against the process capability. They can also assess whether improvements would favorably affect their further processing of the material.

Another important factor is delivery terms. The requirements of JIT for smaller, regular deliveries directly to the production line call for reliable materials and for reliable deliveries. Defective material or irregular delivery will cause shortages, delays, work-arounds, and higher costs in the plant. Suppliers who can count on your business are more likely to accommodate JIT and process control requirements, another argument for long-term relationships.

Once you've found preferred suppliers, a number of reciprocal relations can be established. Worker visits have been mentioned. Joint or reciprocal training can also be helpful. Sometimes, where relations are particularly close and volume or product complexity particularly high, permanent representatives stationed in each other's plants may be indicated. Occasionally, supplier presence goes beyond representation, and a subplant can be established within your plant. Although some companies are secretive, sharing cost information can also allow you to determine which features are worth the cost and which company can best perform some operations in the processing chain.

Another advantage of consistent suppliers is that the disruptions to your work are minimized. This is due to the added attention that you can get from a long-term relationship and because half the number of suppliers means half the number of potential problems. Alternate sources of supply are traditionally sought as a protection against your supplier's failure to provide what you need. But alternate sources also provide an out for the supplier, who knows you do not rely on him. When an apparently better deal comes along, there's no loyalty, and you can be forced to fall back on your alternate sources. Then you get the problems that follow from too much variation in inputs.

If your company decides on a total quality management approach to business, you'll hear and see movement toward single-source relationships with suppliers. You'll get to know the company that provides services or items you use in your own work. You'll get to talk with suppliers' workers almost as if they were in your own company, and they will understand what you are really trying to do. Their abilities can help your work go better, to the benefit of your own customers. Higher quality of input and output, along with more reliable supply, are the results experienced by those who have made the change.

3

TOTAL QUALITY PROBLEM-SOLVING TECHNIQUES— PROCESS AND INVENTORY CONTROLS

If you're like me, you don't want to wait for anything. When you hear of a problem, you want a solution. Then you want to forget all about it and move onto whatever's next. Total quality management is more deliberate and thorough. It produces better, longer-lasting improvements than the quick-fix solutions we're probably accustomed to getting from our managers when we say, "This is your responsibility; solve it!"

As total quality management yields continuous improvements in processes, and consequently in the quality of products, it uses permanent boards and ad hoc teams to bring the skills and knowledge of the workers into the process. These boards and teams, as we discussed in the previous chapter, can provide the company with the information and suggestions it needs to offer better and better products. But simply turning teams of workers loose with orders to "make things better" won't work. Workers, like any of us, need to see why they should seek and make improvements. They need to have some hope that their efforts will yield results and recognition. Workers also need to know what they can do to make things better. They must be trained in TQM processes and committed to total quality.

These structured ways of approaching total quality opportunities are discussed in the next few sections. These sections are relatively short, since their purpose is to introduce methods that can be used and to give enough information so you can conclude whether they might be applied to particular situations in your own company. For most of them, a decision to actually use it will require more detailed research into its nuances and technical aspects. This is particularly true of statistical and other mathematical techniques.

With that caveat, here are some techniques that can be used by quality circles and action teams in discovering and approaching total quality opportunities. These are not all the techniques you might hear of or want to use, but those included have proven particularly effective in the TQM environment. Some of them were devised within the total quality movement and some were adopted by it. As your organization advances in TQM implementation, you will no doubt discover other techniques that will work for you. Use them. One of the great things about total quality management is its flexibility: use and adapt whatever contributes to achieving your goals. Decisions about which to use, if any, or what other techniques might help in a specific situation are, of course, the responsibility of management, the quality circles and action teams, and the total quality facilitators you employ.

NOMINAL GROUP TECHNIQUE

Nominal group technique can be used to reduce unproductive discussion while bringing out the potential contributions of even the most reticent members of a quality circle. It requires some familiarity with its steps and some experience or observation of its application, but it doesn't take a psychologist to use it. It is practical and effective.

Nominal group technique can be used to search for a problem, to search for causes of an already stated problem, or to decide on a course of action. It requires a formal leader to say when to start, when to stop, and to call on members in turn. A recorder may also be useful for tallying ballots when you use written responses.

As the name implies, nominal group technique begins with a group. The group's general objective is already known or is stated at the beginning of the meeting. The general objective of a quality circle is to identify barriers to quality and productivity in a production or service function. Then the quality circle searches for ways to eliminate them. The objective of an action team will be more specific, since the "identifying" part is already done when the team is set up and its problem is assigned to it.

The technique is most effective in stopping unproductive, rambling discussions where many members have something to say about a situation, but none seem to have the underlying facts or a comprehensive solution.

Salient points of nominal group technique are:

1. It elicits the whole group's input on an equal basis.
2. It reserves discussion until there is something concrete to discuss.

3. It produces written, explicit statements of its results and a clear record of its deliberations.
4. It requires a disciplined leader.

I have seen the nominal group technique used successfully to attack a specific barrier to quality and productivity. I have also seen it used to solicit and rank statements that could be incorporated in vision statements, codes of conduct, and mission statements. Perhaps, in its more general uses, you may know it as brainstorming, but the name matters less than the effect. The important thing is that these steps lead to useful, high-quality results with minimum time loss, wheel spinning, and long-winded discourse.

ISHIKAWA CAUSE–EFFECT DIAGRAMS

Ishikawa cause–effect diagrams are sometimes called simply *Ishikawa diagrams* or *cause–effect diagrams*. As you will appreciate when you make or see many of them, they are sometimes also called *fishbone diagrams*. Ishikawa cause–effect diagrams were developed by Kaoru Ishikawa as part of his explication of statistical quality control principles. Because it is not strictly a statistical technique, using no mathematics at all, and because it was developed in the Japanese total quality environment, it has become identified with TQM rather than with mathematical statistics. Statistical techniques may also be TQM techniques, but not all TQM techniques are statistical, and this is one.

Ishikawa lists three types of diagrams, which he views as distinct. I have seen them combined, though, with good effect where circumstances make it a natural thing to do.

The *production-process type* looks like a flow chart, as each activity feeds into the one that uses its output for further processing. In this way, punching a time-card in the factory becomes a factor building up to job cost statements and general financial statements as outputs.

The *cause enumeration type* is different from the production-process type in that it diagrams causes such as "inaccurate hours by job" rather than "punch time card." It also goes further when ascribing causes to the faulty clocking action, such as "pressure on foremen to stay within job limits" or "time clock hard to reach in remote part of shop."

The third type, the *dispersion analysis type*, is a statistician's variant of the production process type. A worker with special training in statistical process control (and you may eventually have many of these) or a true statistician should use them. It's too easy to leave things out or put in the wrong things without proper training in statistics and familiarity with statistical dispersion patterns.

Some of the benefits of Ishikawa cause–effect diagrams are in the discipline they impose. By diagramming the effect and its possible causes, group members are forced to focus on the problem at hand. If the leader uses a board to keep the developing diagram before the group, it will be hard to get off the subject and easy to direct discussion back to it.

Completeness is another benefit, as the discipline required makes it less likely that any possible cause of an undesired effect will be left out. Then, when investigating possible causes to see whether they are actual causes, an Ishikawa diagram and each possibility's likelihood as assigned by the quality circle or action team will direct efforts to the most likely causes first.

Finally, preparing the diagram is an education in itself, since the diagram is a kind of flow chart. It thereby helps all those involved in its preparation better understand their work. When they return to their regular tasks they can find improvement opportunities they would have missed without such knowledge of their service or production process, the uses of its outputs, and its related inputs.

STATISTICAL PROCESS CONTROL

Total quality management began with statistical process control. Recall the seminal work of W. A. Shewhart in the 1920s. Shewhart's methods of statistical quality control came into pervasive use in WWII, as untrained workers entered technologically advanced (for the time) factories making technologically advanced products.

The only way to get this raw work force into action quickly, particularly in view of the number of skilled workers who left for military service, was through extensive, standardized training of workers. Another part of the standardization of products was statistical control to reduce inspection and defect rates simultaneously.

The basic premise of statistical quality control is simple: Reliable, consistent processes produce reliable, consistent products. Reducing variation (improving consistency) among parts reduces variation among completed units. When the process is in statistical control, the occasional parts and units that fall outside the common cause system (those that contain defects) almost certainly have assignable special causes.

Based on that premise, we can use statistical methods to find the units that are no longer identical. This way, there is no need to inspect each part or unit. If sample parts A, L, and Z are in statistical control, and if we have not changed the process during the run, then parts representing the rest of the alphabet have a very high probability of being in statistical control. The probability is so high, in fact, that we need not inspect them all. (Three, of course, is not usually a statistically valid sample size; this is only an illustration of the principle, intended for non-statisticians.)

If we effectively apply statistical control charts, and if our measuring instruments are sufficiently sensitive and accurate, we can detect when a process begins to deviate from its past performance in time to find the cause of deviation. We can then restore normal operation before making any bad product.

How is this magic result achieved? By the use of rigorous statistical methods. A TQM participant must be aware of statistical quality control techniques because their application was a primary source of the entire total quality movement. Another, more practical reason is that statistical techniques are a major means of producing the benefits associated with TQM implementation. To get the benefits, we have to do the work that will produce them. But call a trained statistician for any statistical application in which you have not been specially trained. This book is not a mathematics text or a statistical quality control handbook. Its purpose is to provide an outline of the total quality management process for new practitioners. Highly technical matters should be taught at length by experts.

That said, the following sections will present the basics so you'll recognize the words when your colleagues get into the details of total quality management implementation.

Definitions

Statistical process control is one means of statistical quality control. Another means of statistical quality control is *statistical acceptance sampling inspection*, where the process is not controlled by statistical charts or analysis. Instead, the final product of the process is inspected and tested through a sampling plan. Conclusions about the whole lot of product are then drawn from the sample tested.

Statistical process control is the preferred method in total quality management efforts, since one of the benefits of TQM is reduction of defects, with their attendant costs for rework, scrap, and rescheduling around shortages. Inspection, on the other hand, doesn't reduce defects but merely detects them after they have occurred.

Statistical process control is the use of numeric measurements during intermediate stages of a process to detect and correct deviations from desired outcomes. In an ideal case, where acceptable limits for useful product are larger than the *process capability*, we can detect deviations in the process before they lead to defects in the product. Process capability is the best a process can do when operating within chance cause (common cause) limits. Process capability is determined by examining a process and analyzing its outputs, then charting them. This establishes what the process does as presently carried out. If we want better results than existing process capability, we must change or re-invent the process.

HISTOGRAMS AND PARETO DIAGRAMS

Histograms

When we collect data of any kind, we find values that fall in specific ranges. For example, Table 3-1 shows data as collected. Table 3-2 shows the same data rearranged in order.

Now, if we make a bar graph of these data groups, where the column widths represent the ranges and the heights represent the number of observations that fall in each range, it looks like Figure 3-1. This is called a *histogram*.

Bar charts can also be made where the columns represent things other than data ranges as well. Figure 3-2 shows one taken by the side of the highway showing automobile colors that we observed for a two-hour period.

As you see, the bar graphs allow us to quickly assess the significance and relative importance of counts of large volumes of classified data. Given normal statistical variation, histograms of numeric values typically peak at the data mean and taper off to the extremes. But if the data do not conform to a

Table 3-1. Data Measurements

24	27	25	25	27	28
24	27	22	24	29	25
29	26	28	27	21	22
26	25	26	25	23	25
28	25	30	24	27	28

Table 3-2. Data In Order Of Value

21	24	25	26	27	28
22	24	25	26	27	28
22	25	25	26	27	29
24	25	25	26	27	29
24	25	26	27	28	30

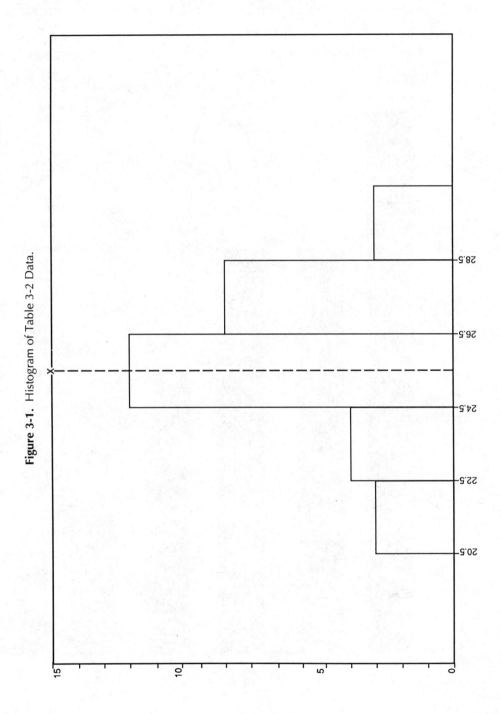

Figure 3-1. Histogram of Table 3-2 Data.

Figure 3-2. Roadside Car Color Frequency Chart.

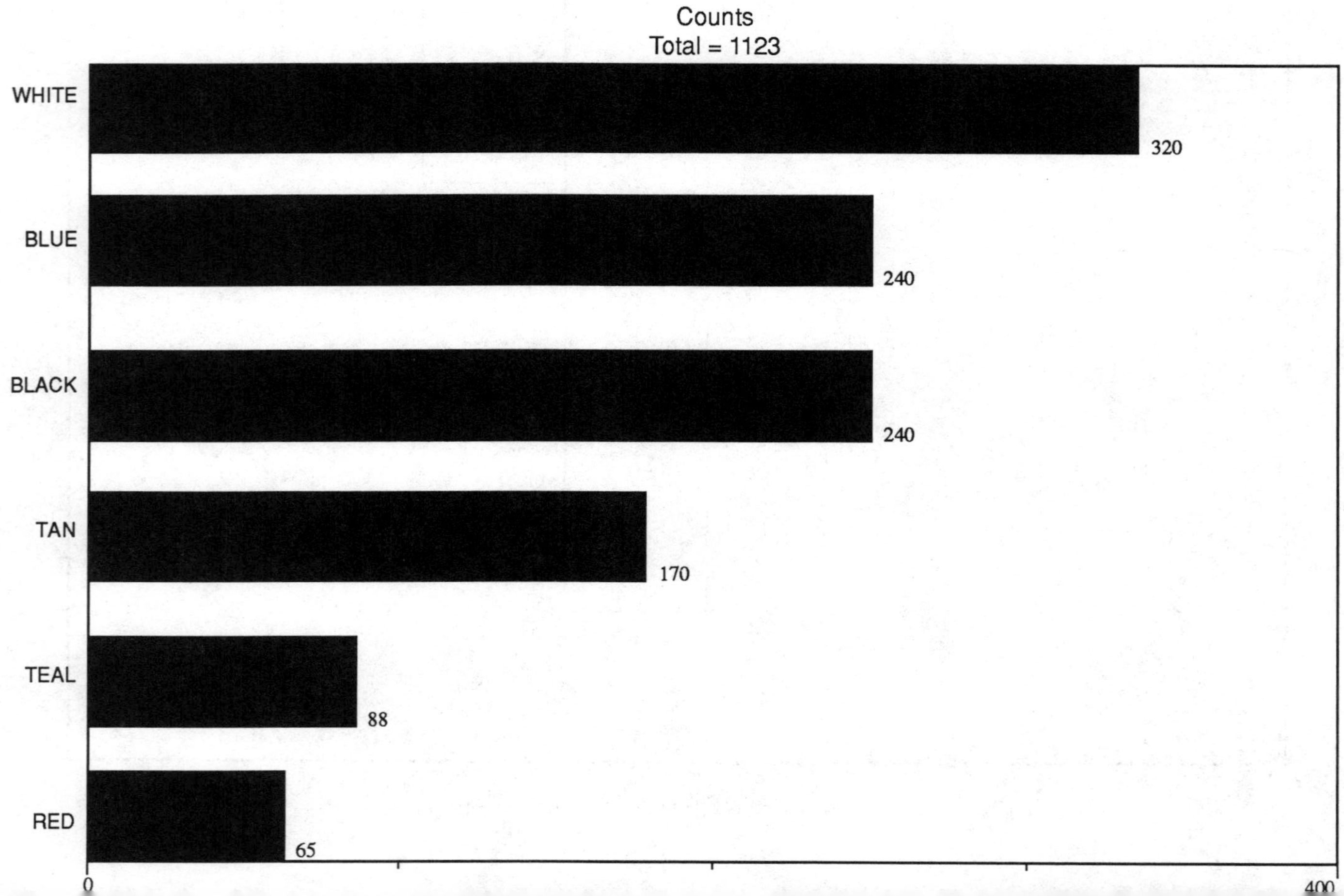

Counts
Total = 1123

WHITE 320
BLUE 240
BLACK 240
TAN 170
TEAL 88
RED 65

standard normal distribution, a histogram (if the sample is statistically valid in size and randomness) will quickly reveal any skewing to one side (see Figure 3-3) or any clustering about more than one peak.

Pareto Diagrams

A *Pareto diagram* is a special kind of histogram. It ranks items by frequency, or, if each item is multiplied by a factor such as cost, by significance. We can use it to decide which problem to attack first. Pareto diagrams are typically arranged with the most significant item on the left and the least significant item on the right so that they can be read in order of importance. Table 3-3 is an example of data on error rates of inventory records, their estimated dollar values, and the resulting total dollar error resulting from each kind of error. A Pareto diagram arranges the same data so that we can see what the most significant inventory error is, as shown in Figure 3-4.

Now, if our quality circle is discussing inventory errors, and we want to know where to start our investigation, we can look at the Pareto diagram and see quickly what the most significant area of search will be, the second most significant area, and so on. Thus, any effort can be directed to the most productive end.

As an aside, you may also have seen that this shows the old *80/20 rule* developed by Vilfredo Pareto, which states that 80 percent of the problems are caused by 20 percent of the items. That's why the 80/20 rule is more formally called the *Pareto principle*.

These histograms and Pareto diagrams are used early in TQM efforts. They are among the first techniques taught and, no matter how much more the workers learn about TQM, they are one of the first steps applied to any discussion item at a quality circle or action team meeting. That's because they are simple, powerful, and focused. They direct effort right to the target.

Table 3-3. Data on Error Rates Inventory Record

Categories	Cost	March	April	May
Misclassification	14.00	27	20	33
Item Cost	5.60	6	9	3
Totals	87.00	13	8	17
Wrong Bin No.	3.70	4	7	1
Item Count	22.00	56	48	72

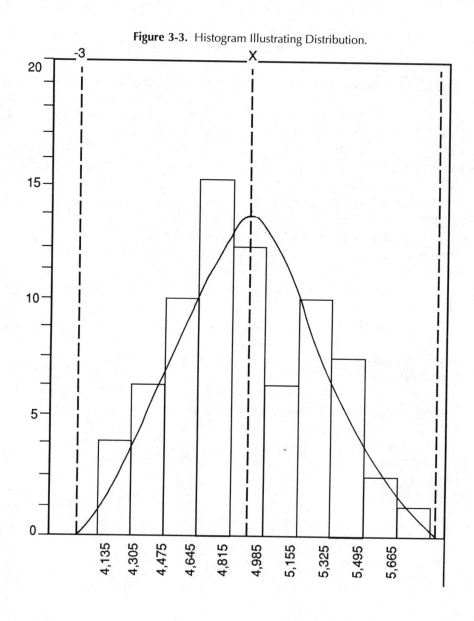

Figure 3-3. Histogram Illustrating Distribution.

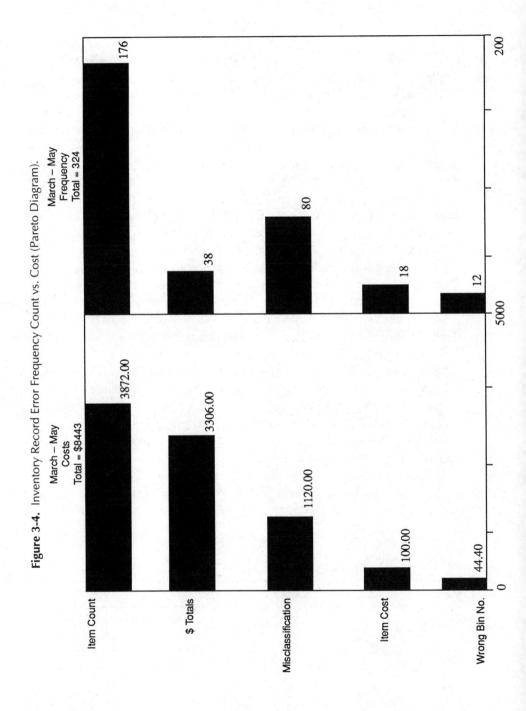

Figure 3-4. Inventory Record Error Frequency Count vs. Cost (Pareto Diagram).

33

X-BAR CHARTS

When any event occurs, there is a desired result and an actual result. The actual results usually differ from those desired. Assuming we always aim for the desired results, the actual values will form a dispersion pattern about the desired values.

For example, when riding a motorcycle in a lane of a highway, we want to stay on a track just left of center, out of the oil slick in the center of most traffic lanes. But if we take pictures from above the road, we'll see the motorcycle wander a bit right and left of that track. And if we take measurements of the positions at fixed times, we'll collect data. We can plot that data on a graph. We'll put the sequence number (1, 2, 3, etc.) of each observation on the horizontal axis and measured distance of the motorcycle from the right side stripe of the road on the vertical axis.

Plotting this data without any other markings gives a scatterplot or scatter diagram. Table 3-4 is an example of some measurements of motorcycle position at different times. Figure 3-5 is a scatterplot of the data.

We can see from this example that even when the rider tries to stay in an ideal position, there is variation. And this variation is random; it has no particular cause within the riding process itself.

"But," you say, "is this good motorcycle riding or bad? How can we tell if the rider or motorcycle changes in some way that affects the process?" Statistics will not tell us whether this is good or bad motorcycle riding. It will, however, tell us when the quality of the riding changes. It does so by establishing the process capability, then detecting deviations in performance from that established capability.

So let's derive some statistics that describe this data. The common statistics are *mean* and *standard deviation*. Mean is just the arithmetic average. Its symbol is X-bar. Standard deviation is a bit more complicated. Its mathemat-

Table 3-4. Deviation in Feet—Motorcycle Position From Right Str.

Sample	Deviation	Sample	Deviation	Sample	Deviation
1	4	8	5	15	4
2	6	9	7	16	3
3	5	10	5	17	5
4	2	11	6	18	4
5	3	12	4	19	4
6	4	13	1	20	6
7	3	14	2	21	7

Figure 3-5. Scattergram of Motorcycle Sequential Position.

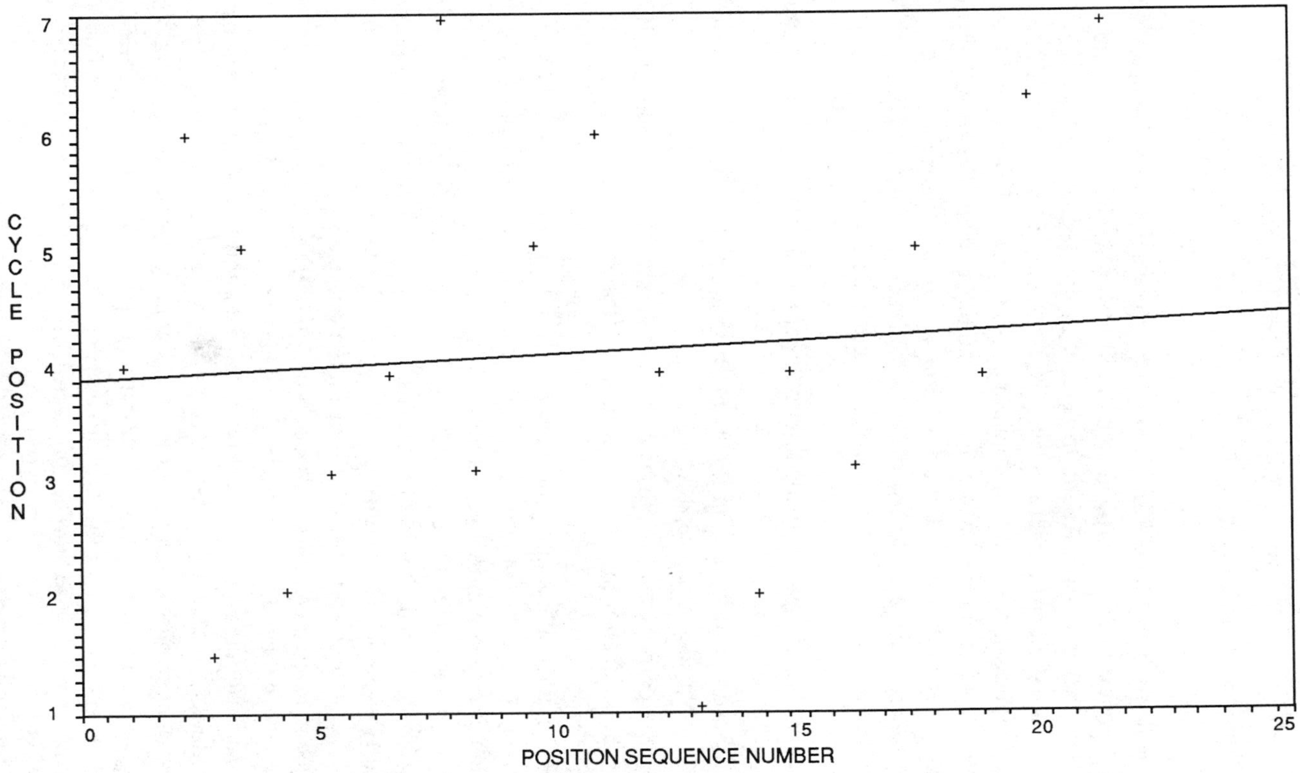

POSITION SEQUENCE NUMBER

CYCLE POSITION

35

ical symbol is σ, or lowercase sigma, and its formula is

$$\sigma = \sqrt{\frac{\sum (x - \bar{x})^2}{n-1}}$$

Mathematicians have established that, if a process is not changed in some way, about two-thirds of the data will fall within the mean plus or minus one standard deviation (σ). About 95 percent of the data will fall within plus or minus two standard deviations, and 99.7 percent of the data will fall within plus or minus three standard deviations. So if an observation yields a value outside three standard deviations from the mean, chances are only three in a thousand that it is a random deviation within a consistent process. More likely, there is a special cause of the deviation.

Some rules of thumb that are often used are:

1. Any observation outside three standard deviations from the mean indicates a special cause.
2. Seven observations in a row on or on the same side of the mean indicate a special cause.
3. Six consecutive increases or decreases in successive plotted observations, even if they cross the mean, indicate a special cause.

These rules do not apply in every case, but they apply in most cases. Your company statistician or consultant will be able to tell what rules apply in any particular real situation you encounter.

The industrial engineer's goal in designing processes is to minimize process variation and to put the process mean as close to the design nominal value as possible. The quality circles' goal is the same. And when deviations justify an action team, the goal is again the same.

One more point should be made. When initially establishing process capability, we expect that whatever the mean and standard deviation of the process turn out to be, 99.7 percent of the data will fall within three standard deviations of the mean. If this turns out not to be true, the process is said to be *out of control*. No analysis or effective improvement can be accomplished until the process begins to produce output that is within some consistent limits, however wide or off of the desired mean. Only a process that is under statistical control can be worked on successfully. So our key points are:

1. Establish process capability by measuring critical dimensions over some span of output.

2. Make a scatter plot of the data. Examine it to see whether one or two points are wildly out of norm. If any are, see whether they are due to faulty measurements or faulty recording of the data.

3. Calculate and plot the mean of the data.

4. Calculate and plot the standard deviation of the data. Typically, though not always, a rule of three standard deviations on each side of the mean is useful for detecting special causes.

5. If an unusual number of initial observations are outside three standard deviations, the process is out of control. Go no further until the process is brought under control.

6. If the process is under control, plot further operations by taking occasional measurements of product. Plot the new data against the mean and range that define the established process capability.

7. If any unusual patterns appear, such as trends, repeated observations on the same side of the mean, or observations outside three standard deviations, stop and investigate the process for special causes.

8. If special causes are found, correct them before making more product.

9. If the process capability is not within desired limits, use quality circles and their action teams to improve the process. It can be improved by changing it to make the mean nearer the ideal value or by reducing deviation about the mean (reducing the standard deviation in subsequent calculations), making it more consistent.

Used this way, charts are the central mechanism of statistical process control. Any worker can use them to control his own work, and can take responsibility for maintaining the quality of his own output. Working in quality circles, workers can discharge the further responsibility of improving their processes and future output.

P CHARTS

After reading the last chapter, an accountant is likely to say, "But my work doesn't give results that can be measured by inches off center. It's either right or wrong. The number of dollars or other units right or wrong isn't really related to the fact that an error has occurred. An error could just as likely be large as small. How can I use statistical methods to evaluate and correct problems in my accounting processes?"

First, it's not entirely true that accounting processes can't be evaluated by scalar measures of values. For example, if the purpose is to determine whether suppliers are paid on time, the lateness of payment can be measured in numbers of days rather than indicating if it is on time or late. Or inventory records can be evaluated by units or dollars of deviation from perpetual records to actual counts. If deviations are more than wanted (probably zero), the processes of recordkeeping, of counting, or of security if stealing is suspected, can be changed. If deviations are irregular, the processes can be investigated to find ways of making them more consistent.

But the question is still valid. Many accounting processes are either right or wrong. If inventory extensions are multiplied incorrectly, they are about as likely to be $1,000 off as $100 or even $1 off. The fact that the error occurred at all is the focus in detecting process problems. The size of the error seems intuitively and from experience to be a matter of chance once it occurs.

Such processes can be evaluated by sampling for attributes. Attributes are yes–no evaluations like "purchase order includes/does not include expected price," "time cards are/are not approved by supervisor," or "inventory is/is not extended accurately." To evaluate such cases, the percentage of items with undesired characteristics must be measured. Thus the name p charts (or *percentage charts* or proportion charts).

In this case, rather than single-point observations, we take regular samples. Then the samples are evaluated for the condition of interest and number of times that the condition occurs; these are used to calculate the percentage of that condition. These percentages can be treated just like scalar measurements in products where dimensions or values other than yes–no are critical elements of quality.

STATISTICAL ABERRATIONS—THINGS NOT TO DO

Mixing Processes

The preceding material on statistical quality control includes a number of points, including that the statistical mean and standard deviation, from which control charts are drawn, apply to homogenous populations. If data are collected on products made by different processes, they describe different populations each with its own mean and standard deviation, and each needs its own control chart. A different process can be the result of using a different piece of equipment, even an initially identical one, because they can vary although they appear identical. Also, if one goes awry the other's data can obscure that fact. So don't lump different processes into a single statistical process control chart.

Hunting the Center

Another way to mess up the data is to keep changing the process. I change the process every time I recalibrate my tooling, so if each time I measure a unit of output, I reset the center of my tool to correspond to any deviation, I am "hunting the center." If the process has not really changed, and the measured variation is merely random, the next variation from the new center has a similar probability of being off center in either direction. So now there are two sources of variation: the normal random variation and the new, systematic variation I have introduced. Since the new, systematic variation is a direct result of the random variation, it will be similar in magnitude. In other words, recalibrating the equipment after each measurement will give a dispersion pattern that is the sum of two patterns based on the same underlying random pattern and will exactly double the variation.

So don't recalibrate after each measurement. Wait until the control charts indicate a probable special cause, then investigate to see what that cause is, then fix it. Don't hunt the center.

Adjusting to the Opposite Side of Center

Another, more volatile adjustment pattern is to adjust to the opposite side of center by the amount of the variation. We can see this where a target shooter hits right, so aims left. If the sights were correct to begin with, he may hit anywhere around his new point of aim. If he then adjusts opposite the bulls-eye by the amount of the next miss, he may occasionally, by chance, hit nearer the bulls-eye. Over time, however, his repeated adjustments to the opposite side of the bulls-eye by the amount of the last miss will result in an unstable pattern. His shots' dispersion grows increasingly large and spreads out indefinitely. As Deming has demonstrated, it looks like the Milky Way with its dispersion of stars stretching huge distances in either direction.

So don't adjust your process "to correct for the miss." Wait until the control charts indicate a probable special cause, then investigate to see what that cause is, then fix it. Don't create a semblance of the Milky Way.

Moving the Target

Finally, there's the situation where we keep adjusting the specifications or process calibration to correspond to the measurements. When this happens, we are aiming at the point of the last hit. I think you can already see what will happen. Once the dispersion pattern begins to acquire a tendency to go in a particular direction, it will continue in that direction as the random variation occurs about a moving target. It's just like the Milky Way illustration in the preceding description, but goes in one direction only rather than in two directions about the nominal center.

Don't adjust your machinery to correspond to the last item measured. Wait until the control charts indicate a probable special cause, then investigate to see what that cause is, then fix it. Don't create even half a Milky Way.

By reviewing these common ways of trying to do the right thing, but really making matters worse, we can learn this lesson: Don't tinker with the production process until the charts say it's broken or you have a specific improvement in mind. After making a process change, either to correct a problem or to make an improvement, establish a new process capability and, again, don't tinker with it until the charts say it's broken or you have a specific improvement in mind.

DELPHI TECHNIQUE

The *delphi technique* had its origin in sales forecasting. The intent was to use the judgment and experience of sales representatives and managers along with more quantitative methods such as statistical regression and economic analysis. Delphi can be used for any forecasting problem or for any problem where the benefits of experience should be added to quantitative analysis.

Delphi is simple in concept, and not especially hard to execute. It is based on the observation that asking people to estimate the temperature on a hot day will get guesses all over the place, but an average very near the true temperature. Allowing estimators to guess again after learning the results of the first round improves both individual guesses and the overall estimate.

There are several steps to the formal process of the delphi technique. First, the quantitative data must be analyzed and a quantitative forecast prepared. Then, a number of alternative forecasts are prepared. A high forecast, a low forecast, and some intermediate possibilities are good choices.

These forecasts are sent to selected experienced people for their opinions, along with a brief on the forecasts explaining what data was used, what action plans may be selected, and what assumptions were made. The delphi group members then select from among the choices, write a synopsis of their reasons for their choice, and return it to the staff analyst for further work.

After the staff analyst has digested the comments, he or she summarizes them and modifies the original forecasts as dictated by the comments received. These are then sent back to the delphi group members for further review. The analyst includes digests of all opinions received, and the delphi group members may change their minds at this time. They then reply with their second-round choices and reasons.

This process may continue through as many rounds as needed to reach consensus, usually three or more. If some maverick group member seems not to converge, that opinion should be carefully reviewed, but may often be ignored as an aberration. If there are two different opinions on which different groups of participants converge, there is probably a reason in their information bases, and investigation is needed.

In a total quality company, the delphi technique can be used to gain participative results where participants are widely separated and it is not feasible to bring them together. It requires a staff analyst as coordinator, however, to make and distribute the original forecasts, to collect replies, and to carry the process through the necessary number of cycles.

Other areas where delphi can be used are for checking strategic plans, assessing competition, and setting prices. It works well for applying judgment to alternatives. It does not work as well for developing those alternatives; groups usually exhibit high judgment but individuals exhibit high creativity, and although the members are separated, the outcome is the result of group judgment rather than of individual ideas.

RE-ENGINEERING

One of the major tenets of total quality management is constant improvement. That seems to imply constant, *small* improvements, but that isn't always the case. Some improvements can be sweeping in scope and effect. When it looks like the old approaches aren't going to keep a company competitive any more and small improvements won't work, it may be time to clear the decks and start over. Starting over is what re-engineering is all about. It means redesigning the organization around the way work should be done, and beginning to do work in that way, rather than just improving the way work is currently being done.

It means less of doing things better and more of doing better things. Just as a product can be re-engineered to use single extrusions or castings instead of assemblies made of many parts, an organization can be re-engineered to use one worker or one tool to produce a set of data or other outputs.

Looking at products, a redesign can be effected with both utility for the customer and producibility for the company in mind, using teams representing various disciplines. Customers or internal users of products can be included in the redesign through team membership or market research techniques.

Sometimes, whole organizations need to start over and remake themselves. Usually they do so only in response to overwhelming evidence in the form of losses in the marketplace (though a few, like 3M, have been able to do it by growing new lines of business and closing old ones as they go along). That's why so many old companies (like U.S. Steel), with firmly established cultures that have been successful in the past, fade in an ever-changing marketplace. A case in point is IBM. It has been forced to reduce its size because it didn't keep up with the changing marketplace and didn't develop the products, processes, and organization to serve the emerging customer requirements that increasingly moved away from IBM-serviced mainframes. Instead, building on IBM's popularization of its disk operating system (DOS), others have given us PCs, networks, and minicomputer integration for productivity improvements that the old approach could not have provided. It appears IBM is now redefining itself in response to this competition. That redefining process will probably include organizational re-engineering.

It is important to note that TQM does not, by itself, require re-engineering an organization. In fact, re-engineering an organization establishes a whole new system whose process capabilities will be unknown. Re-engineering is to be avoided where continuous improvement in the old processes will still yield major results. But where returns from continuous improvement are running out of room for further development, a better return may be available by taking a fresh look at the whole company—its structure, products, and processes. Then it's time to start over with a new, better product, process, or organization.

PROCESS VALUE ANALYSIS

Process value analysis (PVA) is used in a total quality management implementation to accomplish the two primary objectives of TQM:

1. Satisfy the customer.
2. Eliminate waste.

Like all TQM tools, PVA is data driven and customer focused. It uses information derived from measurement and worker participation. The sources of input information are:

1. "Close to the customer" techniques such as focus groups, customer visits, surveys, and other market research.
2. Employee involvement techniques such as quality circles.
3. Performance measures such as cost, cycle time, and scrap rates.

To carry out process value analysis, customer requirements are traced back through the production process and compared to the cost of meeting those requirements. At the same time, activities are identified that do not directly produce a thing, service, or feature that the customer will pay for. In manufacturing, marketing defines what the customer is really trying to do when buying a product. The customer requirements are passed to engineering.

At this time, a fully implemented total quality management effort will typically form a multi-disciplinary team from marketing, sales, design engineering, manufacturing engineering, manufacturing operations, customer service, finance, cost accounting, and administration. Except in very large development projects, these members do not all serve full time. This team develops a product that meets customer requirements, will work, is producible, is maintainable, and is within customers' price limits. Validation techniques are also applied using prototypes before going on to full-scale production and sales. In meeting cost objectives, the proposed production processes are examined to see which of them yield features the customer values.

Process value analysis also detects processes and steps that, by their nature, cannot add value for the customer. An example would be if you were storing product between production steps and keeping records of labor applied. These things may be necessary, but the customer doesn't care whether you do them or not.

By applying process value analysis at the beginning of the product design stage, a truly cost-effective product can be made with no wasted costs. If a product is already designed, in production, and being sold, the opportunity to get in at the design stage has been missed. But PVA can still be used during consideration of redesigns or engineering changes.

For products in production, the same procedures can be applied, but the changes that can be made may be restricted to the manufacturing processes and associated activities. It should also be noted that although this discussion describes products as though they are hard goods for external customers, the same process value analysis procedures apply to less tangible products and to products for internal customers.

Given that we can't reinvent our company or many of our products overnight, how do we perform process value analysis on our existing products, whether they are internal products or ultimate products for outside customers? There are five steps:

1. Identify your business processes.
2. List the activities involved in the processes.
3. Determine which are *value-added activities* (which the customer would pay for).
4. Identify the causes of costs (sometimes called *cost drivers*) in both value-added and *non–value-added activities*.
5. Identify opportunities to eliminate or minimize non–value-added activities.

Beyond the process value analysis, itself, remain the steps of figuring out what to do to reduce non–value-added activities.

Once we have identified candidates for reduction or elimination, we can use other TQM techniques to achieve that reduction. For example, we can reduce inspection and rework through statistical process control, which can catch an incipient bad product before any actual bad product is made. We can reduce material handling through just-in-time inventory management and through manufacturing cells. If we have speeded our production process enough, we can reduce accounting costs through *backflushing*—recording material and other costs in a single entry after the product is finished, rather than through many entries to a work-in-progress account. Also, we can reduce set-up costs through a single-minute exchange of dies.

Wherever the process value analysis starts, finding non–value-added activities can lead us to reduce activities that do not contribute to the usefulness of our products in the customer' hands, thereby freeing resources to make less costly or more feature-laden products, or both. This gives us a competitive advantage.

BENCHMARKING

Through total quality management, an organization can look at its processes to find product quality problems along with any difficulties that workers may be having meeting product specifications. But what if the product quality and specifications seem to be acceptable but competitors are offering better products or lower prices? We can find out how they do it by first finding an organization that produces the product better and cheaper than anyone else. This process is called *benchmarking*.

There are two types of benchmarking:

1. Benchmarking the product.
2. Benchmarking the production process.

Process benchmarking is also called *best practices* because the most effective process contains the best ways of doing its component tasks. Like a benchmark that is used as a standard for a worker to measure a product's dimensions, benchmarking in total quality management provides standards derived from examining the best products and processes we can find. Benchmarking yields both a standard of performance and methods of meeting that standard.

There are a number of benchmarking techniques available. We can take apart the competitor's product and see how it's put together (i.e., we can see how close the tolerances are and how much variation there is among units and among parts of those units). Another way is to ask them. It seems odd, perhaps, but competitors are sometimes proud to be asked about their processes and will be willing to share some information. A competitor's supplier (especially if they're also our supplier) will offer us the same kind of product they offer the competitor, if asked. I'm not talking about stealing secrets, just about specifying materials and services of the highest quality, like those our competitors are getting. It's not out of line to ask a tool supplier what kind of equipment they sold a competitor or what training package they offered with it. If the competitor uses the tools in a proprietary process, it might be out of line to ask a tool supplier to reveal that process, but the tools themselves and the terms of sale are not industrial secrets.

Sometimes you can find other companies that use processes like yours for making non-competitive products. For example, nearly every maker of small appliances uses an assembly department. Exchange visits between groups of workers from a forklift maker and a golf cart maker are not at all competitively threatening. Both can be winners.

Finally, the easiest way to improve through benchmarking is to look within your company for other plants or departments that are doing what you do, but doing it better. If what they do can work for you, use it!

USING MANUFACTURING CELLS AND GROUP TECHNOLOGY

Manufacturing cells are like little factories inside a factory. In a big factory, there are usually many departments or shops, each with a defined function. There might be a receiving department, a raw materials storage facility, a milling shop, a lathe shop, a plating shop, an inspection department, a finished goods warehouse, and a shipping department. Each manufactured unit has to go through each department. If the units are made of many parts, each component has to go through many steps by itself, then come together in an assembly department.

This kind of processing involves many movements of material, with attendant risks of loss or damage at each move. In addition, there are usually delays in each shop before work on the material is started and again when it's done before it can be moved onto the next shop. There are factories where the aisles are nearly blocked with staged material awaiting movement or processing. All this stuff lying around or blocking aisles is work-in-process inventory that had to be paid for.

Industrial studies have shown that over 90 percent of processing time can be spent waiting to move, moving, and waiting to enter processing again. If that time and movement could be eliminated, inventory in process could be drastically reduced, factory floor size could be reduced by eliminating certain aisles and waiting areas, some material handling equipment could be eliminated, personnel could be reassigned, and customers could get their orders faster. One means of eliminating material movement is to line the machines up in order, so a part can move directly from machine to machine. Another change that results from using manufacturing cells is that workers commonly learn all the tasks in the cell or even processing each part through all its steps. The workforce then becomes multi-skilled. The benefits of specialization are also retained, but each worker is a specialist in the items that are commonly processed in his cell rather than in the machine type used in his shop or department, which would have processed virtually all the items in the plant. It can be thought of as vertical rather than horizontal specialization.

Another gain to the company is that many set-ups can be eliminated since machines no longer process many kinds of parts. When the parts processed are the same or similar, set-up time can be eliminated since the machine is left in its production set-up all the time. If changes are needed for different, but similar parts, the changes are often to tools and fixtures of similar size and type, simplifying the set-up.

Scheduling is also much simpler since none of the intermediate moves have to be scheduled. Once an item is scheduled into a cell, it will be started and processed to completion as a single continuous process. Thus, most of the headache of plant scheduling simply goes away.

Cells need not process only a single part. A cell can process a number of items sequentially if they are sufficiently similar. How do we figure which items are enough alike to be processed efficiently in the same manufacturing cell?

The answer is with group technology. Briefly, *group technology* is the grouping of items according to the technology required to produce them. I have seen two methods of grouping such items: computer-oriented codes that identify the machines used in making each item, and a more visually oriented matrix. Both methods are intended to do the same thing—sort items into groups that can be processed in cells.

If you're in a manufacturing industry and your company is involved in total quality management, manufacturing cells are sure to be among the solutions considered when quality circles and action teams look for ways to improve the company's processes.

If you're not in a manufacturing industry, you may still find application for the principles of manufacturing cells, but they will be fewer since you are probably less dependent on the finite capacities of production machines. All the same, look at your offices. Could work flows be arranged to be more linear, with less walking around? A TQM implementation will eventually bring you to that question.

USING SELF-DIRECTED WORK TEAMS

We are all aware of the traditional structure of organizations, where each member reports to someone above. In contrast, in the hotly competitive environment of today, "flatter" organizations that can cut costs and improve response attract increasing interest. *Flatter organizations*, with fewer layers of supervision, are possible only if spans of control can be increased. One way to increase spans of control is to allow more freedom to subordinates at each level. In fact, the term "span of control" should be replaced with "span of cognizance" or "span of communication."

In total quality management implementations, workers are given proper training, and the missions of the company are clearly stated. With the ability to do their work and with knowledge of the purpose of that work, subordinates can be allowed to work without close supervision. Of course, communicating goals and plans, checking, reporting, and occasional redirection are still needed. Close, constant supervision, though, can be reduced. Since each superior spends more time communicating and less time giving detailed instructions downward and detailed reports upward, managers can assume responsibility for larger organizational units. Thus, we have a flatter, lower-cost, more responsive organizational pattern.

A result of the change to more communication is that work units begin to require less and less direct supervision. In some cases, the change has gone so far that first-line supervisors have disappeared. Work units have become *self-directed teams*. They have a leader to serve as a focus of communication, but the leader does not give orders. Decisions are made by the whole group.

Such groups may decide on changes in methods. They can requisition needed material and tools. They request capital equipment when needed. They even make hiring decisions. They assign tasks within the group and trade tasks at their discretion. Non-performers are "counseled out."

Such groups look like little companies within the company; they even look a bit like clans or tribes. Since each looks like a little company, each can formulate its own vision statement (who we are, what our values are) and mission statement (what we do within the larger unit's mission). It can develop individual job missions and task definitions if it likes.

Of course, teams cannot be allowed to run amok. They must still be given clear goals and proper training. Product specifications must be furnished. Instructions for the work, training in basic skills, engineering assistance, and similar resources must be available as before. In fact, such organizational support becomes more important. The difference is that after initial instruction, the team decides what help it needs to make a quality product with minimum variation from unit to unit.

Problems can arise when an individual would rather be judged on his own work than on the team's results. Teams can also get into trouble when they become too insular and get a "them" and "us" feeling about other teams, especially those upstream or downstream from their part of the total production effort.

Self-directed work teams sometimes seem to result from other aspects of TQM, as well-trained workers in quality circles and action teams take responsibility for their own output and as they improve the products they pass to their customers. They can also lead to other aspects of TQM since they require proper training and usable mission statements to guide their work. If properly trained, they will communicate with their internal suppliers and customers to improve their performance.

Not all total quality companies will create self-directed work teams, and those that do will not necessarily have them everywhere in the organization. But where they are used they are both a contributor to and a consequence of the TQM effort.

SINGLE-MINUTE EXCHANGE OF DIES

Single-minute exchange of dies is another translation from Japanese to English. Another name for it is *one-touch changeover*. The idea is that a machine and the set-up worker are not producing actual product while the machine is being converted from making one thing to making another. Reducing set-up time can save real money. Large set-up costs, when put into production lot–size formulae, dictate large lot sizes, and large sizes mean large dollar amounts tied up in inventory, both during manufacturing as work-in-process and later in finished goods. When production equipment can be changed among items instantly, production lots can be limited to a day's requirements.

Reducing set-up time also calls for simpler set-ups, with simpler fixtures and set-up guide devices replacing complex fixtures and separate measurements. The result is more dependable calibration. And less variation in set-up means less variation between lots. In other words, it means higher quality products.

Some common factors in successful quick-changeovers are:

1. Design simple fixtures and tools.
2. Set a goal for the workers.
3. Ask the workers to think, try, think, try, until they achieve the result they want.
4. Use a fixture on only one machine—even nominally identical machines and fixtures differ.
5. Devise positioning guides for dies and fixtures to eliminate repeated measurement.
6. Pre-position fixtures and dies near their machine.

You can see that these factors correspond to total quality principles in that they call for simplification, they involve the workers, and they eliminate sources of variation.

JUST-IN-TIME INVENTORY CONTROLS

Just in time (JIT) is another of those English idioms adapted from Japanese. The Japanese word is *Kanban*, meaning roughly the same as the English *trigger*. Inventory control is what kanban, or just in time, is all about. In its strict sense, it is an inventory control or material control method and only that. The expansion of the term's meaning resulted from the order in which ideas were introduced to different people.

If you're a material- or inventory-oriented person, you may have come to your interest in total quality management and its accounting aspects through the American Production and Inventory Control Society. That organization uses the term *Just in Time* or *Kanban* to mean the whole approach and set of techniques that is elsewhere called total quality management, total quality control, or similar names. We needn't be distracted by this; we need only remember it when reading the literature and talking to other practitioners.

Traditional inventory control systems emphasized stocking levels. Their goal was to keep just enough around to meet production needs, reordering at a point where a balance of storage costs, ordering costs, volume price breaks, and "safety stock" made the inventory itself least costly to keep. You may remember the terms "economic reorder point" and "optimum stocking level" from school. But the classic formulae for these levels do not take into account the costs of spoilage, damage, and the purchasing function itself. (Or, if the cost of purchasing is accounted for, it's on a deceptive basis, as the accounting section of the book will point out.) It also assumes that costs of storage and movement are unavoidable. Just in time starts over with new assumptions about which costs and risks are avoidable.

The goal of more modern inventory control methods is to eliminate costs of movement, storage, and obsolescence. Just in time also eliminates clerical costs of reordering material and keeping records of its location, quantity, and shelf life. JIT carries a risk of its own, though, in its reliance on supplier dependability. Let's see how JIT changes inventory control practices through its elimination of traditional stocks and storage.

As noted in the sections on linear, continuous process manufacturing (manufacturing cells and group technology), reducing movement and storage between operations cuts movement costs, storage costs, spoilage risk, space requirements, and the investment in stored goods lying around a facility awaiting their next operation. Just in time advances the inventory avoidance effort one more step, from the producing company back to the supplier. It reduces or even eliminates inventory held in the incoming materials area and in raw materials inventory. It does this by having suppliers make deliveries of material each day, sometimes several times a day. These materials are not stored at the facility, but are delivered *just in time* as they are needed for further processing. When manufacturing cells are arranged in U-shapes or straight lines, and aisles are provided for material delivery, inventory can be brought directly to the part of the production process where it is needed.

Another source of dollar savings and reduction of damage risk is achieved if suppliers don't package and preserve parts. Unless items are particularly delicate or will be transported long distances, they can be delivered in trays, cartons, or other containers that allow them to be used immediately, with no need to unpack them to prepare for use.

If enough doors are provided at a plant, material can be brought in directly by the suppliers' deliverymen and placed where it's needed by using the aisles rather than winding through the manufacturing facility. Incoming material, except in special cases, is neither counted nor inspected by the customer before using it. This requires special arrangements and trust between suppliers and customers. Recall from the section on working with suppliers that such relationships are a necessary part of a TQM implementation. The savings that can result from such relationships, both in quality and in inventory costs, make it very rewarding.

Since the user of material does not inspect or count it before beginning to use it in production, the material must be assuredly of proper quality. Quality is assured through total quality relationships with suppliers. Each supplier of material provides a statistical control chart with each delivery, often simply placing the chart in the box with the parts.

If there is no material stored in a plant, and if it is delivered in small batches as needed, how does the supplier know how much to bring and when? The answer lies in the Japanese word *kanban*. The kanban, or trigger, was developed at Toyota Motor Company where the whole system was first created as a means of notifying suppliers that more material would soon be needed. It was simply a piece of paper put in the box, bin, or tray with the parts being used. When the worker came to the kanban, he put the paper or card in his outgoing mailbox, pneumatic tube, or other delivery means to start it on its way back to the supplier. When the supplier received the kanban, he knew to deliver another batch to the workplace where it was needed.

Today, paper kanbans are not the only kind used. Sensors connected to lights in distant locations and computer links back to suppliers are other ways to achieve the same goal. The important thing is that suppliers know when to bring more material. The new material will also have kanbans in it to notify the supplier when the next batch is needed. The kanbans will be placed so that sufficient lead time is available for picking, staging, packing, and delivering what's needed.

If the cycle for preparing a batch of material is longer than the cycle for using it, there may be a number of kanbans for the same item in process of being filled. This occurs because while batch 1 is in use, and batch 2 is in work to replace it, batch 3 must be started. The need to work one or more batches ahead is more acute when suppliers manufacture directly for the customer's production needs.

Kitting

A variation on just in time is *kitting*. Kitting is the practice of putting all the parts needed for an operation together before delivering them to the production process. This can be done on form-fitting, vacuum-molded trays so that refilling the kits consists of merely filling the fitted slots in the trays. Kitting is gaining increasing acceptance and, in some companies, is treated as an old idea—just the normal way of doing business.

Kitting has also been used successfully in rework applications. There, all the parts that *might* be needed to rebuild an end item are in the kit. Some parts are always replaced in rebuilding, but some are replaced only if the worker finds she needs it. By providing all likely parts, the kit reminds the worker of what should be examined and provides the means to do the work. This also adds to quality, as workers don't spend hours waiting for parts and don't pass items along due to too little time to get replacements for marginally unsatisfactory parts. Rework kits are not completely used because they provide all likely parts, but not all will be needed. The partially used kits are returned to a material department where they are refilled for the next use.

A similar process has been used when "consumables" like small fasteners, safety wire, clean rubber gloves, or lubricants are needed by each worker. These can be provided in prepared trays or boxes for the employees. When the worker is off, material personnel on another shift can refill each person's supplies case so he starts the next day with a full consumables kit. Again, the temptation to get by without proper material is reduced and "waiting and fetching" time lost by skilled workers is also reduced. Productivity for the company and job satisfaction for the worker are the usual results.

While kitting for production, kitting for rework (with partial kit refills), and consumables kits are not in themselves JIT, they are highly successful and productivity-enhancing offshoots of it. These techniques can be, and frequently are, used within total quality management companies as part of their customer response, product quality, and worker talent utilization emphases.

MATERIAL REQUIREMENTS PLANNING

After reading the section on just in time (JIT), you may be thinking of ways to use it in your business. But it sometimes happens that we envision a stream of identical material coming to our processes to replace material that has been used. We then realize that our production processes don't use large amounts of identical material. We may be a custom or job shop.

What does total quality management have for operations where each unit is unique? If each unit is a variation on a basic model, it may be possible to stage all likely parts together, and allow the worker to use those needed, even if not the same for each unit. Or it may be possible to make up kits containing all likely parts, returning unused parts of kits for use in new kits. Both these methods have been used successfully. If you find them helpful to you, you will discover that JIT principles still apply.

In other cases, though, the production process looks more like a set of related, but different projects. Each uses a unique bill of materials or other resources, and sending a kanban to replenish material wouldn't work because no one could easily know what would be needed for project B at the time the components of project A were delivered. When a kanban goes in a tray of parts, we don't know what the kanban should tell the supplier (or internal supplier department) to bring next because the next product will be different. An answer has been developed in the technique called *material requirements planning*, or MRP.

In principle, MRP is really easy. Whenever any one of us does a simple job at home we begin with production planning—we decide what we're going to do and what steps or procedures we will use to do it. Finally, we figure out when we can do it. Then we figure out what items or supplies we need, making a bill of materials for the job. Now we have a one-job production plan, schedule, and bill of materials.

Material requirements planning consists of putting together many such plans from within a facility and scheduling the necessary material to arrive exactly when needed. Its goal is the same as just-in-time inventory techniques: to reduce storage, movement, risk of damage or obsolescence, space requirements, investment in inventory, and lines at material issue points. The difference is that rather than being demand–pull from production, MRP is a supply–push from scheduling. The goal is the same as with JIT, though: to see that the worker finds the materials he needs arriving in the workplace when they are needed. MRP is used with custom and unique products because the worker can't ask for what he'll need the way a JIT kanban does for him. He doesn't know what he'll need until he already has the job to do. Even if he does, he hasn't efficient means to ask for it. Those are the jobs of production and material planners.

Material requirements planning starts just like the home job in the example (but on a more extensive scale) with a production schedule and bills of materials. If the jobs are so unique that there are no pre-defined bills of materials, the MRP definition is expanded to include creating them.

Looking at the production schedule and working backwards through order and shipping time (and supplier manufacturing lead time for custom items) gives order dates for each item needed for the production plan. These items are consolidated so that orders are placed for such quantities as the plan calls for within a given time period, such as a month. But delivery dates under an order may be staggered to fit production schedules. By bringing material to the plant only at the time it's needed, MRP can achieve its objectives of minimizing the amount of storage and movement of material. If this seems like common sense to you, you're right. But then why are our plants so often full of material in storage, being moved, or piled up awaiting further work?

MRP sounds easy because it's an easy concept, but it is difficult in actual practice because of the complexity of even a modest production effort. If several independent efforts are going on at the same time, as when a plant reworks 16 airliners of four different types, the process complexity becomes overwhelming. Effective computer systems are the only practical alternatives. Computers can handle the complexity reliably, if they are properly programmed and if their users know what they're doing. There are also a number of computer programs offered for purchase.

To review, the steps of Material Requirements Planning are:

1. Customer order.
2. Engineering specification and bill of materials.
3. Production schedule.
4. Material requirements consolidation for all jobs in a time period.
5. Schedules of material arrival.
6. Material order.
7. Follow-up, in case of changes or delays.

You've probably noticed by now that just as material and components are resources that are used in any productive effort, so are time, tools, and facilities. What about these items? Can they be scheduled too?

As you have guessed, they surely can be scheduled. A set of tools for scheduling resource units that includes material, but that goes beyond material alone, is *manufacturing resources planning* or MRP II. You'll quickly see, however, that resources planning is not limited to manufacturing.

MRP II incorporates the production planning parts of our earlier discussion into the formal system, beginning back at the first step with the marketing plan and the resulting sales forecast. Subsequent steps are also addressed by MRP II, typically in a series of distinct modules. They may be:

1. Forecasting.
2. Engineering.
3. Master Scheduling.
4. Bills of Materials.
5. Material Requirements Planning.
6. Facilities or Capacity Planning.

7. Labor Scheduling or Shop Floor Control.

These modules could each be implemented independently, and since beginning all of them at once would be overwhelming, they do not all work together the first day of implementation. They are, however, highly interdependent.

CONCLUSION

The important thing to remember as your organization begins its total quality implementation is that you are likely to see many of the techniques discussed in this chapter considered for use. They may be adopted, adapted, or rejected in any combination that makes sense. But one of the advantages of total quality management is that it isn't proud. Techniques like just in time (JIT) that originated in a TQM atmosphere, can be used with techniques like manufacturing resources planning to bring about the best effect for each organization. The cooperative process of finding a need for improvement, finding ways to improve, and putting those ways to use is what makes total quality work.

PART II

UNDERSTANDING COST ACCOUNTING

The first part of the book was devoted to the accountant (or anyone else) who is involved in total quality management implementation, and who wonders "What is this TQM stuff, anyway?" This part of the book is for managers (or anyone else) who are involved in total quality management implementation and who wonder, "What is cost accounting, anyway, and can it be of any use to me in total quality management?" Part II also offers something to experienced cost accounting professionals in its presentation of new or neglected accounting methods such as direct costing, activity-based costing, and cost of quality.

4

INTRODUCTION TO COST ACCOUNTING

Cost accounting was developed to serve managers whose enterprises have outgrown their ability to remember everything. A sole proprietor at a medieval fair, for example, probably knew what he paid for each item and knew what it cost him to live, and that was enough. But as businesses get larger, they become more complex in two ways: they have too many people and operations to keep track of by personal observation and they have more than one activity or product. How can an owner keep track of it all? How can individual managers keep track of things in their departments?

Financial accounting and cost accounting became two distinct ways of keeping track when outside owners wanted to know about performance of the whole enterprise, but managers of component parts of the enterprise needed to know about their own products, departments, or projects. *Financial accounting* reports are those described in newspapers and in annual reports. Financial accounting shows the result of everything the organization did, all together, expressed in dollars to aid in *investment decision making*.

Cost accounting shows the results of each thing the organization did, separately, also expressed in dollars, but often including other measures, such as total units produced. Cost accounting information is used for *management decision making*. It is more directly connected to action. When a manager sees performance of his organizational unit compared to budget or to past data, he has a guide for action. The categories of cost tell where to look for reasons for good or poor performance. They can be a guide to what can be changed to improve performance. In total quality companies, the quality circles and action teams can use cost accounting information to help in their tasks.

The mechanics of accounting are fairly simple. Transactions are recorded in *journals* and assigned accounting codes. The amounts are then *posted* to *ledgers*, where all amounts with a particular account code can be added together to give a total for each time period, each department, each job, and so on. The totals from the ledgers are then entered as lines on *reports*. So that's it: record in journals, summarize in ledgers, and communicate in reports.

Of course when there are thousands or millions of transactions and when different managers clamor for different breakdowns of information, the job becomes much harder. When it's not entirely clear whether a building is used mostly for storage or for production it calls for judgment. When a single item or action benefits several projects or time periods or both, it may call for negotiation among managers. If accounting is simple in concept, it is not easy or simple in application. Messy or complex businesses can be reflected accurately only in similarly complex accounting processes and products. In most cases, the accounting system mirrors the organization it monitors.

DEFINING COST OBJECTS

There are many reasons for cost accounting, but the main ones are centered on assigning costs either to outputs or to organizational components. The unit for which we collect costs and to which we assign them, whether a unit of output or an organizational unit, is the *cost object*.

Assigning costs to outputs as cost objects allows us to know what each thing or service unit costs. Assigning costs to organizational units as cost objects allows us to concentrate on organizational performance. We can determine who is causing costs to be incurred, report those costs to the unit responsible, and allow the management of that unit (and the workers, in a total quality company) to act on the data reported.

The first area to cover is assignment of costs to products, and we begin by asking, "What products?" Before designing a cost collection system to determine the cost of any output, we have to know what that output is. Do we want to determine the cost of our ultimate product only? If so, we need only assign costs to that product.

But it's not quite as simple as it first appears to answer the question "Cost of what products?" There are ultimate products delivered to the organization's customers, to be sure, but there are also intermediate products. Some intermediate products, like parts, can simultaneously be end products as replacements and intermediate products as parts of assemblies. Finally, there are internal products that the company's customers never receive. They are such services and items as inspections, performance reports, personnel actions, kit assembly, and equipment maintenance that are used within the company.

One final point about products as cost objects—after costs are collected and aggregated in one way, with accounting codes that group them, it is almost impossible to break them out again. For example, if we collect costs of screws by coding labor on the thread-cutting machine to "labor" and also labor on the device that makes the hexagonal keyway in the screw head to the same account, "labor," we can no longer easily answer a question about how much of the cost of the screw is thread-cutting and how much is keyway forming. I make this point to emphasize the importance of determining what the cost objects are before beginning the cost collection process. It's easy to collect costs any way managers want them, but once they are collected, that's the only practical way they can be reviewed and analyzed.

The other commonly defined kind of cost object is an organizational unit. We want to know how much products cost, like a dishwasher, if that's our product, or an hour of legal research, but we also want to know how much it costs to operate the personnel department or the plating shop, regardless of how many or how few articles are actually processed.

Of course, after figuring the cost of operating a functional department or shop, we also will want to look at quantity of output; that will tell us something about efficiency. It won't tell us everything though, since the department supervisor is typically not responsible for the amount of work he is given to do or for the capital equipment he has. TQM can do something to change that, and certain accounting practices can also discern "non-responsible" costs elements. Outputs as cost objects and departments as cost objects are not exclusive—they work together for certain kinds of measures.

When gathering costs for departments, many of the same questions arise as when gathering costs for units of output, and for the same reasons. Before we can collect costs for a department, the department must be defined. Is it important to get total administrative costs, accounting department costs, accounts payable processing costs, or voucher review costs? The more finely the costs are broken down, the more cost codes the system will need, but the more detailed the information will be in the end.

Like output costs, department costs can be easily broken down at the information system design and information gathering stages. They are very difficult to break out after the information has been gathered and summarized. So again, cost objects should be defined during accounting system design.

There is one more general kind of cost object that is more like a unit of output, but partakes of the nature of a department as well. Jobs or projects are often used as cost objects, especially in construction or production facilities where materials are processed in lots that move through their processes as a single bundle of units. Large-scale service projects like consulting engagements, legal engagements, or product sampling activities are also accounted for as jobs. Job costing applies to any work with a defined start and end, and that uses resources that can be readily distinguished as applying to one job among a number of jobs.

Where jobs are cost objects, workers commonly record time to jobs, materials are assigned to jobs, and equipment usage is also charged to the jobs. Sometimes costs that apply to jobs but are not easily computed, like copies made or telephone charges, are assigned through electronic devices that record job codes, or they may be assigned based on short-term studies that are presumed representative of total activity.

One advantage of jobs as cost objects is that it allows for cost-plus pricing, where a company charges its customer for time, materials, a contribution to overhead, and a negotiated profit percentage. Another is that it provides data for use in future bids. It can also be used in TQM applications for a statistical chart of cost elements among jobs to find statistically significant deviations. The causes can be sought for remedy if unfavorable, or for emulation if favorable.

To summarize, then, *cost objects* are products, departments, or jobs for which costs are to be collected and summarized by unit. Units for which costs are collected are items (for products), departments or shops (for departments), and projects (for job costing). The cost objects must be defined at the design stage of accounting system development, or detail will be lost in summary and it will be very difficult to break out cost components. Reporting can be done by item, department, or job.

COST ELEMENTS AND COST ALLOCATION

If we assign costs to units of output, we know what each item, report, or service unit costs us to produce. If we assign costs to operating units or staff functions, we can find the cost of operating a subdivision of the company or a department. Each kind of information has its uses. Which we want depends on whether we are looking at production processes (for products) or operating processes (for departments). Industrial engineers involved in production planning will look at product costs. Department managers will look at department costs.

Whichever we are costing—products or organizational unit operations— there remains the question of what cost elements are of interest. Should we collect the cost of labor in a single number or should we distinguish direct production labor from supervisory labor and from support service labor? Does anyone care what rent for the building costs once the lease is signed and we can no longer change it? Are travel costs of interest only as a whole, or should airfare, cab fare, and hotels be separated? (The Internal Revenue

Service insists that entertainment and meals be separated from other costs since they are only partially deductible for tax purposes.)

Whatever we decide, the totals we make in our ledgers are made for each cost object, such as lots, jobs, or departments, and also for each cost element, such as labor, benefits, travel, occupancy, depreciation, utilities, and whatever else may be of interest to management. Usually, cost elements are set up on the company's ledgers as distinct *accounts* with unique numeric *account codes* and cost objects are set up as if they were little companies within the big company, each having the relevant cost and expense accounts replicated. Thus, each transaction will typically require both an account code and a job or department code to be properly recorded.

Some of these costs are specific to each unit of output. For example, direct material (component parts) can be traced to specific final assemblies. These are usually accounted for in job lots for small items that are produced in lots, but for large, high-value assemblies such as aircraft, ships, or buildings, materials are charged directly to the final product. In process industries like chemical or paper making, inputs may be charged to a production lot.

A refinement occurs for continuous processes that are never turned off, like certain brewing, steel, or paper making processes. In these cases, the amount of product made in each time period is treated as a lot or batch, even though there is no exact cut-off of product flow. Amounts remaining in process at the period end are accounted for as work-in-process.

For the moment, though, we need only recognize that costs of inputs going directly to a specific unit or batch of output can be charged directly to that unit as cost elements of that cost object. These elements are typically direct labor and direct material.

You see that it's easier to assign some costs to departments than it is to assign them to products. That's because some costs, such as supplies and telephone, either cannot be traced to single units of output like parts can or, like supplies, they may be traceable but are not worth the bother. Whereas costs like direct labor and direct materials that can be traced into specific units or batches of output are *specific costs*, costs that benefit many units or batches and are not worth tracing to each one benefited are *common costs*.

Where common costs occur in the production departments, they are usually called *production indirect* and where they occur in staff or management functions they are usually called *general and administrative* or *G&A* costs. Both production indirect and G&A can be called *overhead*, and because it could mean either or both, the term "overhead" is usually not used in technical discussions.

Where common costs are assigned to products, the procedure is called *absorption costing* because the common costs are "absorbed" by the products, at least on the accounting records.

In absorption costing, production indirect costs are assigned at the department level, and G&A costs are either assigned within departments or at the end of the production process. Since such costs cannot be readily traced directly to a unit of output, they are usually assigned along with another cost that can. Some examples of cost assignment bases are direct labor hours, direct labor dollars, or material dollars.

This kind of cost assignment according to some algorithm is *cost allocation.* So when an accountant speaks of *allocated costs* he or she often means costs that are really not caused by the product or other cost object, but that have to go somewhere. The apparently arbitrary nature of such allocations is one of the complaints that operating personnel have long directed at accountants, and that TQM can help address. Just how that can be done is the subject of the last part of the book. For now, we're still exploring cost accounting as commonly practiced.

So now we have three terms to deal with in absorption costing: *cost objects* for which we collect costs, *cost elements* that describe the costs incurred by or for that object, and a new one, *cost allocation* for assigning common costs using *allocation bases* as the algorithm for spreading common costs of production indirect and general and administrative (G&A) to products.

Let's see how simple we can make cost allocation principles. Believe it or not, the federal cost accounting standards that apply to military contracts make a lot of sense (even though the Defense Contract Audit Agency (DCAA), doesn't always use them sensibly). If your business has defense contracts, you'll need to know about the standards. If not, they don't apply to you, but they are still a fairly good statement of sound allocation principles.

The standards say, essentially, that if a cost can be traced directly to a product or batch that benefits from it, it should be directly assigned to that product or batch. If a cost can be traced to a group of products, it should be allocated only to products in that group. If a cost benefits only one department or function, it should be included in the costs of that department and allocated only to products worked in that department. If a cost benefits only a business segment, it should be allocated only to products of that segment.

The federal cost accounting standards also recognize that some costs, particularly G&A costs, may have no clear, preferable basis of assignment, and they may be assigned according to any reasonable basis. Finally, federal cost standards require that whatever is done about cost allocation, so far as discovering what products or departments should absorb them, must be done consistently. To protect our national treasury, the standards state that consistency must apply across the company's whole business so that the federal customer doesn't get a disproportionate share of common costs.

It may sound complex, but the worst is over. We have covered just about all there is to the concepts of absorption costing. An alternative is *direct costing*, which is seldom used in actual businesses, but is theoretically preferable. We will discuss direct costing in a later section.

COST-VOLUME-PROFIT ANALYSIS

Cost-volume-profit analysis (CVP) is sometimes called *break-even analysis*, but "break-even" is really only one point on the continuum of possible profits or losses that can be found by this technique. It's conceptually simple, but powerful in that any model of organizational performance that uses accounting data is a generalization from, or a special case of, CVP.

We will examine CVP because it is a useful tool and, even more importantly, because it contains many of the basic economic relationships that cost accounting data go into, and do so in fairly understandable form. Although there are many refinements and adaptations to specific situations, the principles we learn from cost-volume-profit analysis are most of what we need to know to use cost accounting data effectively.

The underlying idea is that net profit may be positive (profit) or zero (break-even) or negative (loss), and that it is equal to revenue minus costs. But whereas revenue generally equals unit price times units sold, costs do not necessarily equal nominal unit cost times units sold. That's because while some costs vary according to units made or sold, others remain the same no matter how many or few units may be sold.

Let's look at the components of this simple equation,

$$\text{Revenue} - \text{Costs} = \text{Profit or (Loss)}^*$$

Now let's examine the components of this relationship one by one to see where it can be improved.

Revenue and Profit

We usually think of revenue as units sold times price. For a single product, without options or variations, offered at a fixed price, take-it-or-leave-it, this may be a valid assumption. But in fact, even a single product may be sold for a while at one price, then the price may be lowered to sell more.

Note: Accountants generally put negative numbers in brackets or parentheses. They're easier to see when scanning than are minus signs.

For example, we may have a store selling socks. We sell all the socks we can at $5 a pair. When sales begin to slack off, we offer a special at $4 a pair, and sales pick up again. Adding a cost of $3 a pair, we see that we make more profit on the $5 sales, but more total profit by accepting $4 sales as well, after all $5 sales have been harvested. As long as succeeding lower prices remain above cost, profit increases. A special case arises where no more sales can be made above cost. Here the problem is minimizing losses on remaining sales; anything we get is better than throwing the socks away. We see such end-of-season or discontinued model specials all the time.

In economic theory, the ability to offer different prices to different buyers is called *segmenting the market*. As long as buyers can be kept from crossing the lines and buying in another market segment (which airline passengers try to do), it maximizes revenue. Segmentation may occur over time, as in the socks example, or by other qualifications like excursion fares.

The point is that revenue is not necessarily a straight line function, though we can think of it that way to help understand what cost accounting is all about.

Variable Costs

In the example cited in the previous section, each item was bought at a certain cost and sold at a particular price, resulting in a profit or, sometimes, a loss. The total cost of the items sold varied exactly with their number.

The costs that vary directly with sales or with output are called *variable costs*. They do not always vary one-for-one with production, but they nearly do so in most cases. Variable costs are typically those that go directly into the product, such as materials, direct labor, and certain consumable supplies used in producing the service or item. These are the things that you use if you produce a unit of service or product, but don't use if you don't produce one.

Fixed Costs

But you are no doubt aware that not all costs change that way. In a retail store, it's possible to imagine a case where there are few costs that do not vary, as where employees are paid commission only and rent is a percentage of sales, as in a mall. But usually there are costs that we pay no matter how much or little production occurs. These are *fixed costs*.

Fixed costs are paid no matter what. They are such items as rent (usually), supervisory labor, supplies, and the cost classes often called *production indi-*

rect and *general and administrative* (G&A). Recall that both may also be called *overhead*.

Production indirect costs are incurred directly in the production facility or process, such as supervisory labor, inspection, equipment depreciation, facility costs, equipment maintenance, and shop supplies. G&A costs are incurred in support departments such as executive management, personnel, travel administration, accounting, finance, and marketing. G&A costs are not really fixed, of course, but they change in response to management decisions or such external factors as tax or regulatory changes, not in direct response to production volume. With respect to cost-volume-profit analysis, therefore, they are fixed costs.

Semi-Variable Costs

Some costs that are treated as fixed for simplification purposes do vary with volume, but only through indirect effects. Such costs may be personnel, where more job changes occur when we are doing more, or accounting, where more transactions and jobs must be accounted for, or purchasing, where more material is needed. But they do not vary directly, since they have some component of their total that is there however much or little is produced in the operating departments.

Even in operating departments, some apparently variable costs do not vary directly with volume. For example, labor may be more or less fixed at 40 hours per employee for low volumes, and seldom be less, since "busywork" can be found. Labor will increase at high volumes, though, as overtime becomes necessary. Only if lower volumes look permanent will layoffs occur to reduce the fixed portion of the cost.

Selling costs may be a classic mixed or semi-variable cost, as they have a fixed component of base salaries and administrative costs and a variable component of commissions.

The basic idea remains valid, though, and understanding it gives the key to most microeconomic and cost accounting analysis.

All this is very interesting and powerful if applied to actual situations, altering the classification of costs as fixed or variable to suit the real circumstances and altering the order of calculation to answer the question being asked. With lots of refinements, it's nearly all of what cost analysts do.

But a word of caution is also needed. Remember Deming's question, "How do you know?" in the section describing total quality management and its practices. It implies that no analysis is worth more than the data that goes into it. Only data that accurately reflects the organization's actual activities and operations can give useful analyses.

BUDGETS AND STANDARD COSTS

Budgets are used as a way of comparing actual costs to a plan, the budget. *Budgets* are applied to time periods or to projects that have definite beginnings and endings. Many of us use monthly budgets at home. The budget is compared to actual expenditures to see whether we are behaving the way we thought we would. Changes in the plan or changes in our behavior are possible to make sure our goals are met.

Standard costs are notional costs, usually the best estimate we can make of what actual results will be, that can be used either like a budget (and can be thought of as a product budget) for evaluating actual results or that can be used instead of actual costs for certain accounting processes. Standard costs differ from budgets in two ways: they apply to units of output, rather than to time periods, and they can be used in the accounting system instead of actual costs for certain transfers and cost allocations. This way, we don't have to wait until a time period is over to get actual costs for assignment to products or to other departments. Differences (called *variances*) between actual and standard costs are either charged directly to income or are carried over to become part of the next recomputation of standards.

So there are two uses of standard costs: as a performance measure and as an administrative convenience.

Types of Budgets

Do you have to go through an annual budget process at your company? Do you have marketing budgets, sales budgets, and operating budgets? Many companies do, as a way of translating their operating goals and plans into numerical terms. Such numbers can later be compared to information that is gathered on the actual performance of the organization and its departments.

For a whole organization, the budget process consists of a *master budget* that reflects the total expected activity of the company for a set time period, usually a year. The master budget consists of three components: the *sales budget*, the *capital budget*, and the *operating budget*. Most of this chapter focuses on the operating budget, but first let's look at the sales and capital budgets.

When a company makes its business plans, it starts with a marketing plan that tells what it will do to find customers for its services or products. The effect of the marketing plan is assessed and a *sales forecast* is derived. Often, the sales forecast becomes the sales or revenue budget without further change, but often some "windage" is applied before translating the forecast into one or more sales budgets. The "windage" reflects management judgments of what can be achieved or what should be used as performance targets within the overall forecast.

Capital budgets are plans for spending on long-lived equipment and facilities, for buying or selling lines of business, and for getting the resources for doing so through securities offerings or borrowing. A capital budget is longer term than sales or operating budgets for two reasons: long lead times to plan, design, and build capital equipment and facilities on the expenditure side or to register securities and negotiate loans on the resources side, and the long life of items placed in service as part of capital allocation. Consequently month-to-month variations are less valuable as performance measures. Capital budgets are therefore usually quarterly or even annual rather than monthly.

Operating budgets allocate limited resources to achieve overall goals. They provide a guide for action during the daily execution of operating plans, ensuring that each function in the organization has the resources it needs and that none expends resources that are needed elsewhere.

Of course, circumstances change, and budgets can change with them. It's the requirement to consciously change the budget that imposes discipline on an organization, as resources must be obtained to carry on added effort in any particular area. Such resources can come from changing plans in another area (cutting someone else's budget), borrowing or capital stock sales (capital budget), or from within the department in question (realignment of line items). But they must come from somewhere, and the budgets ensure that total spending will stay within total resources.

A *project budget* also has a beginning and an end, but not defined as equal blocks of time. The project doesn't go on and on; it ends completely when the project is finished. Consequently, it is not organized into monthly blocks, but presents the whole project at once. Of course, time periods are also possible in project budgets, but they are mainly to keep the project on schedule and to provide along-the-way check points. Time periods in project budgets do not by themselves define the resource expectations.

Both department and project budgets can be used in the same company for different purposes. A construction company would have department budgets for administrative functions but project budgets for each building under construction. An equipment manufacturer might have department budgets for general and administrative functions but separate project budgets for large custom machinery. At the same time, such a company could use production budgets with standard costs for smaller standard products.

An adaptation can be used where there are both fixed and volume-related costs under a single manager's control. The *flexible budget* includes some costs, such as facilities charges and supervisory labor, at fixed monthly rates. Other costs, like direct labor and direct material, vary with volume of output.

They are shown on budget reports as output multiplied by a budget (or standard) cost per unit.

Flexible budgets allow valid comparisons to plans where the manager is not responsible for the variations in output, as where sales differ from budgeted amounts, so amounts of service or production also vary. By using a flexible budget, we can look at the results in such departments without the need to recast the budget for each fluctuation in output demanded.

Another type of budget is less interesting for the current purpose, but should be mentioned. The *cash budget* is a translation of sales budgets, capital budgets, and operating budgets into cash flows. Inflows from normal sales, securities offerings, and borrowing are compared to expenditures for capital goods and operations. Any needed adjustments are made to payment schedules and borrowing plans, and the resulting cash budget is used to ensure that enough money is on hand to pay suppliers, employees, dividends, and so on. A cash budget allows problems to be detected early enough to adjust plans so everyone can be paid and excesses can be invested for the best returns.

We discussed how budgets are computed, but there are two refinements that deserve mention: *continuous* or *rolling budgets* and *zero-based budgeting*. Continuous budgets are not made once for a whole year, but are added to each month, so they always display the budget for twelve months (or some other time horizon) in the future. As a month is completed and drops off the beginning of the budget-to-actual reports, another is added to the end. This provides continuous review of performance plans, and is especially useful when three-year or five-year plans are in place. The monthly plans, as expressed in the budgets, can be kept in line with long-range plans and as variations occur, later plans can be changed to keep intended future performance in line with the long-range plan.

Continuous budgets also allow a manager to see his expected performance farther in the future and manage today for both today and tomorrow. He can more easily think about what actions today will affect plans tomorrow. He can ask for changes in the plans where needed, but only if he knows what the plans are. A continuous budget tells what future plans are, so changes can be started early enough to be carried out in an orderly way.

Zero-based budgets are a useful way of asking, "Do we really need to do this at all?" and, "How much of this is worthwhile?" Unlike the usual budget calculation that begins with last year's amounts or the last similar project's figures, a zero-based budget has no base to start from. Each cost budgeted must be derived from an operating plan that begins with no assumptions about what will be done. The process being budgeted is reviewed as though it were a new program.

You may remember that when former President Carter was elected, he inaugurated zero-based budgeting in the federal government as a way of ensuring that each program was thoroughly reviewed from the bottom up. This was one idea that really did some good. The problem was that bureaucrats soon learned to play that game too, so it lost some punch. In addition, building a federal program budget from zero is a lot of work for the staff and for the review echelons, so it wasn't done as effectively as it might have been. Even in cases where no changes in total budget occurred, the managers were forced to justify their activities and therefore to ask, "Should we do this? At what level? If we want to keep these resources for our programs, how might they be more effectively used?"

Most of the benefits of zero-based budgeting can be gained by occasional reviews, perhaps each three or five years. It's possible to avoid throwing the whole organization into turmoil by having different departments or plants undertake their zero-based budgeting cycle in different years, so the workload overall remains more or less constant from year to year.

To recapitulate, then, budgets are operating and financial plans translated into dollars. Budgets may be for a continuing activity, divided into time periods, or they may be for a one-time project. Budgets are compared to actual results as one measure of whether plans are being executed as intended. Although we usually think of operating budgets for expenditures within a project or department, there are also sales or revenue budgets, capital budgets, and cash budgets. Some variations are flexible budgets and zero-based budgets.

Standard Costs

Deming, you may recall from his point, "Eliminate numerical quotas," was against performance standards measured numerically for two reasons: they make the worker feel pushed to meet an artificial standard rather than to produce quality service, and they become a level that is "good enough." Although his words in this point do not say so explicitly, I know from hearing Dr. Deming at length that he included an end to standard costs. He believed in measuring actuals only. Some TQM companies have done just that.

At some risk for disagreeing with such a distinguished man, I believe that Dr. Deming misapprehended what standard costs are all about. If his misapprehensions are shared by the workers, though, he may still be correct in his view of the motivational effects.

Standard costs serve two purposes, as mentioned earlier: they can be used for transferring costs through the production system from serving departments to using departments without waiting for a period to end so actual costs can be calculated; and they can be used by management as a way of seeing whether reality corresponds to plans. In fact, they can be charted on statistical process control charts so that managers can see whether a seemingly low-cost or high-cost job or month is within normal statistical variation (a likely result of common causes) or is a peculiarity (likely to have a special cause) worth investigating.

In total quality implementations, each organization will have to make its own decision about whether and how to use standard costs. But in order for the non-accountant reader to become acquainted with them, let's look at standard costs more closely.

Standards may be set as ideal standards, attainable only under ideal conditions. If they are, we risk Dr. Deming's fear coming true, that workers can reach them so seldom that they become discouraged and give up trying to make any improvements. Another problem with ideal standards is that, since they are seldom attained, variances are almost always negative; thus, the use of standards in lieu of actuals to simplify cost transfers becomes unrealistic. They are not a good substitute for the actuals.

Standards may also be set as an estimate of actual costs to be incurred. They may be set just a little tight, but at an attainable level. One way to derive such costs is to use the mean of past costs (a component of the process capability discussed in the TQM part of the book under statistical process control). If the company wants to make the standards a little tight, the statistical analysis will also yield a standard deviation that can help in deciding how much better than the mean is reasonably attainable within the variation of common causes.

Standards can be compared to actual costs in the type of statement shown in Table 4-1.

Why is it beneficial to use standards? We've already mentioned administrative convenience in transferring costs from cost centers (departments) to other departments or directly to products. Other reasons are:

1. They allow management by exception. It's not necessary to react to every variation in organizational performance, since they are clearly laid out and a judgment is possible as to whether to investigate further.
2. They can be used for projections and forecasts in managing cash and inventory balances. They can also be used in department budgeting.
3. If attainable, they can be a spur to performance.
4. They aid in *responsibility accounting*, to be covered in the next section, as each cost is assigned to the manager who can affect it.

Units Produced 11,000
Units Scheduled 10,000

Table 4-1. Cost-Report—Standard vs. Actual I
June

Cost Element	Standard				Actual				Variance
	Per-unit Quantity	Price	Per-unit Budget	Total Budget	Per-unit Quantity	Price	Per-unit Cost	Total Cost	Total Variance
Labor	2.30	$16.35	$37.61	$413,655	2.20	$18.12	$39.86	$438,504	($24,849)
Material	5.10	$3.26	$16.63	$182,886	4.90	$3.25	$15.93	$175,175	$7,711
Total Direct Costs	7.40	$19.61	$54.24	$596,541	7.10	$21.37	$55.79	$613,679	($17,138)

What's wrong with standard costs?

1. It's not easy to decide whether a deviation from standard is material and worth investigating. Statistical process control techniques can help here, though, and will be covered in the final section of the book.

2. By setting a standard that will be easily interpreted as "good enough," they allow complacency. There is no incentive to improve beyond the standard. This is one part of Deming's view.

3. As a further incentive to inefficiency, workers who see that they will be measured by the standard soon cease to improve. They fear that management will raise the standard if they do, but not increase their pay or psychic rewards. "No matter what we do, they just want more out of us!" This is the other part of Deming's view.

4. Management by exception leads to negative reinforcement only, where poor performance brings down an army of investigators, but great performance brings only tighter standards.

5. Concentrating on cost performance through easily seen standards leads to neglect of other measures of performance, like customer satisfaction and timely processing of orders.

As we will discuss in the last part of the book, which integrates total quality management and accounting, most of these disadvantages can be ameliorated or eliminated by TQM principles. We can share the information with the workforce; we can use statistical process control methods to present it as a way of detecting causes of significant variation rather than as a way of "keeping on the backs" of the first-line supervisors and workers.

Budgets and standard costs are really the same thing, then, but budgets are used for organizational units or distinct projects, whereas standard costs are used for units of service or product. If efficiency remains constant, budgets vary with the length of the time period or the size of the project. Standard costs, when accumulated, vary with number of units produced.

Both can be used for performance assessment. If consistent methodology is used (what the statistician would call a *system*, using the word in a special technical sense), statistical process control techniques can help decide both budgets and standard costs. The statistical variation can help distinguish between likely common causes and likely special causes.

In addition, standard costs can be used instead of actual costs to transfer costs from service providers to the benefiting organizational units. This way, it's not necessary to wait for month-end to calculate actuals for transfer and the benefiting managers' units know what they'll be charged for services whose costs are beyond their control.

Cost Variance Analysis

One more topic deserves to be covered in the discussion of budgets and standard costs. How do we know where to look for causes of variation? The answer is that favorable or unfavorable *variance* can be analyzed to break out component parts of *total variance* as *usage, efficiency,* or *quantity variance* (how much we used), *price variance* (what we paid), and *volume variance* (a special case where we allocated overhead in amounts different from plan because we changed the number of units produced).

Some total quality management practitioners feel so negatively toward standard costs that they consider breaking down variances as making things worse. But, as we've seen, this mostly stems from a misunderstanding of what standard costs are about. If that misunderstanding is shared with the workforce and first-line supervisors, that's another argument for education and training within TQM, not an argument for eliminating all standard costs.

In any event, the purpose of this chapter is to introduce non-accountants to budgets, standard costs, and the variances that arise from comparing budgets and standards to actual performance. Whether a company should actually use these as management tools is a decision that each company must make for itself.

How do we break down variances? We begin by looking at the standards. If you've ever made a budget, you recall that you looked at the number of resource units needed, field sales representatives, for example. You then multiplied that number by the cost of each unit, say $4,100 per month, including benefits and payroll taxes, but excluding commissions. In each case where total costs had to be estimated for a project or a month of operations, you multiplied the amount of resource needed by the cost of that resource. You did it for component parts, personnel, and material.

If overhead costs were allocated to the thing whose cost you budgeted, for instance a house in a real estate development, you also budgeted the allocation of costs based on an estimate of the total production indirect overhead or general and administrative overhead and an estimate of the total consumption of items constituting the allocation base.

The same calculation shown for a product could also be used for a project or a service or for a department for a month or year. The only remaining piece is to calculate the components of total variance: usage and price variances. Table 4-2 shows that calculation.

It's not essential to understanding the concepts of variance analysis, but sharp readers (probably engineers; they notice everything mathematical) may have picked up the fact that calculating price and usage variances separately, then adding them, does not yield total variance. That's because there are actually three components to the total variance: excess units times standard price, excess price times standard units, and excess units times excess price. Put

Table 4-2. Cost-Report—Standard vs. Actual II

June

Units Produced
11,000

Units Produced 11,000
Units Scheduled 10,000

	Standard				Actual				Variance: + (−)		
Cost Element	Per-unit Quantity	Price	Per-unit Budget	Total Budget	Per-unit Quantity	Price	Per-unit Cost	Total Cost	Usage Variance	Price Variance	Total Variance
Labor	2.30	$16.35	$37.61	$413,655	2.20	$18.12	$39.86	$438,504	$17,985	($42,834)	($24,849)
Material	5.10	$3.26	$16.63	$182,886	4.90	$3.25	$15.93	$175,175	$8,172	$539	$7,711
Total Direct Costs	7.40	$19.61	$54.24	$596,541	7.10	$21.37	$55.79	$613,679	$25,157	($42,295)	($17,138)

another way, the added units consumed (if the usage variance is unfavorable) must be multiplied by the added price paid (if the price variance is also unfavorable), giving a *cross-variance*. We eliminate the cross-variance problem by multiplying excess units by standard price to find usage variance, but multiplying actual units by excess price to find price variance, essentially assigning the cross-variance to the price variance. Don't worry if this is too difficult—it's not essential and most accountants are not aware of cross-variances either.

The last variance is *volume variance*. You're probably tired of all this algebra-in-words by now, so let's make this one easy. Volume variance arises from overhead allocations. Let's use production indirect overhead as an example.

If a shop was to produce 100,000 units of output and to incur $250,000 of production indirect costs, $2.50 would be allocated to each unit produced. But if only 90,000 units are actually produced, only $225,000 ($2.50 × 90,000) will actually be allocated to products. So no matter how exactly the shop hit its target for using resources and paying budgeted amounts for them, there is still $25,000 in production indirect cost that is unallocated. This $25,000 is volume variance.

You can see that volume variance is merely a way of explaining what happened to certain costs that should have been allocated to products under an absorption costing system, but were not allocated because plans changed. It has no significance for measuring efficiency of fixed cost (assuming indirect costs to be fixed) incursion, but is a mathematically necessary component of total variance to "explain" why expected indirect and G&A cost absorption did not occur. The example cost report is shown again in Table 4-3, this time with volume variance added.

If volume variance is too hard to deal with for the benefit you see in it, don't worry about it. Later we'll see that a method called *direct costing* is more in keeping with economic theory and that volume variances do not occur when using it for management purposes.

Although analysis of variances is difficult to grasp, it does yield useful results. If the budgets and standards are merely an accounting convenience for assigning costs, they show us where our estimates are off and might be considered for adjustment in future periods. If the budgets and standards are also performance measures, the variances tell us where to look for operating events that differ from expectations. Either way, they can be useful to managers and to quality circles or action teams in total quality companies.

RESPONSIBILITY ACCOUNTING—DEFINING THE RESPONSIBLE PARTY

One of the purposes of accounting is to tell us how we're doing. Accounting has an advantage over most other measures in that it expresses its measure-

Table 4-3. Cost-Report—Standard vs. Actual III
June

Units Produced 11,000
Units Scheduled 10,000

Cost Element	Standard				Actual				Variance: + (−)		
	Per-unit Quantity	Price	Per-unit Budget	Total Budget	Per-unit Quantity	Price	Per-unit Cost	Total Cost	Usage Variance	Price Variance	Total Variance
Labor	2.30	$16.35	$37.61	$413,655	2.20	$18.12	$39.86	$438,504	$17,985	($42,834)	($24,849)
Material	5.10	$3.26	$16.63	$182,886	4.90	$3.25	$15.93	$175,175	$8,172	$539	$7,711
Total Direct Costs	7.40	$19.61	$54.24	$596,541	7.10	$21.37	$55.79	$613,679	$25,157	($42,295)	($17,138)
Indirect Costs (Per-unit amount = Indir budget/units schedule)			$22.60	$226,000	(Indirect applied = per unit amount × units produced)		$22.60	$248,600	Volume Variance	($22,600)	
Total Cost			$76.83	$82,541			$78	$862,279	$235,157	($42,295)	($39,738)

Note that volume variance, added in the last illustration, has no price or usage components.

ments in consistent units, namely, dollars. Thus, it is possible to compare the performance of different organizations and parts of organizations.

Of the two main approaches to accounting, financial accounting is directed to the whole enterprise and, therefore, is used for public reporting and corporate loans. Investors are interested in financial reports. Cost accounting looks into the organization and reports on its component parts. Managers are interested in cost reports. When cost reports are used in conjunction with some basis of evaluation, such as a budget, past performance, or industry averages, it becomes a performance report.

One of the ideas that has come with total quality management is that individual workers are usually not the cause of observed results. Rather, the system within which they work produces common causes and occasional unexpected events produce special causes. Individuals are part of the system but except in a few malicious cases or cases of true incapacity, they are doing their best. Problems usually come from inadequate job definition, training, product specification, tools, or material. (Recall the first part of the book when we talked about statistical process control and about common causes and special causes.)

Each of us who has been a manager, though, has been responsible for the performance of our organizational unit in the sense that we are answerable for it. If performance is not what is desired, we are the ones who must initiate a search for common or special causes and we are the ones who must make change possible. Given all that, the name *responsibility accounting* still sounds like a way of blaming foremen and supervisors for their units' performance. However, it is really intended as a tool for them to manage their operations.

We have all seen cases where a subordinate manager is compelled to give lengthy explanations to successively higher levels of management for apparently poor organizational performance, diverting his attention from actually making a difference in the operation. Such cases would be said by a "new model, modern manager" to represent a misuse of accounting information by putting an individual on the spot rather than putting a problem in the spotlight. Cost accounting is intended to point out where operations might be improved, not to give ammunition to shoot at people. So perhaps "responsibility accounting" is a unfortunate name and something like "segment accounting" would be better, but "responsibility accounting" is the name that is generally recognized.

Since each organizational segment has its supervisor or manager, that is the person who is said to be responsible for the performance of the segment. If you are already involved in TQM and if it has taken a "soft" turn in your company, you may prefer to think of the whole group as responsible for its performance, especially if self-directed work teams are used. It really doesn't matter, because we will come out with the same accounting result and use the same accounting methods in any case. The accounting methods we will use for reporting the results of its operations to each unit, in consistent dollar terms, are those of responsibility accounting.

When we talked about cost objects earlier, we saw that an organizational segment, such as a shop or department, can be a cost object. When we collect and report operating costs for such an organizational segment, we are engaged in responsibility accounting.

Responsibility centers can be, and usually are, arranged hierarchically, so that a business unit's chief officer is responsible for all revenue, costs, and facilities under his cognizance, and hence of the profitability of his part of the enterprise. In small and middle-sized companies, where there is only one business unit, this is typically the president.

The chief executive of a business unit has marketing, sales, finance, personnel, and operations under his cognizance. He will want composite reports on the whole unit as his own report card, but he will also want reports on the performance of the departments in his unit. The subordinate managers will also want measures of their subunits, such as work sections or shops. A hierarchical reporting structure might look like Table 4-4.

As we've discussed, the idea of responsibility for different kinds of performance, overall profitability, costs only, or various combinations, as well as for the expenditure of funds for capital investment are all included in responsibility accounting. There are thus three main kinds of responsibility centers:

1. *Cost centers* have no control over or responsibility for revenue, but are measured solely on their costs. Cost centers may be operating units like plating, shipping, warehousing, or customer service. They may also be internal service departments like accounting or maintenance. Either way, they have no easily recognizable revenue, and must be measured against such yardsticks as budgets or other units' performance.

2. *Profit centers* are units that are responsible for the entire revenue cycle, from marketing and sales through production or operations to shipping and customer service. They are measured on their overall results. In some large companies, there can be profit centers for products or brands, where the revenue is measured against costs of manufacturing and distribution, but the manufacturing and distribution are not controlled directly by the brand manager. Instead the brand manager constructively "contracts out" those functions to internal manufacturing units and pays an internal transfer price for them. In such cases, the transfer prices become revenue to the manufacturing and distribution arms, and they are profit centers too.

Table 4-4. Responsibility Accounting Hierarchy

Chief Executive Level

Responsibility Centers	Budget	Actual	Total Variance Fav. (Unfav.)
Sales	X	X	X
Production	$732,500	$743,000	($10,500)
Engineering	X	X	X
Accounting	X	X	X
Total	$1,336,000	$1,299,000	$37,000

Production Department

Responsibility Centers	Budget	Actual	Total Variance Fav. (Unfav.)
Material Handling	X	X	X
Machining	$487,000	$495,000	($8,000)
Plating	X	X	X
Assembly	X	X	X
Total	$732,500	$743,000	($10,500)

Machining Shop

Responsibility Centers	Budget	Actual	Total Variance Fav. (Unfav.)
Sanding	X	X	X
Milling	$97,000	$96,000	$1,000
Numerical Control Machining	X	X	X
Grinding	X	X	X
Total	$487,000	$495,000	($8,000)

Milling Operation

Controllable Costs	Budget	Actual	Total Variance Fav. (Unfav.)
Direct Labor	X	X	X
Direct Material	$52,000	$54,000	($2,000)
Production Indirect	X	X	X
Total	$97,000	$96,000	$1,000

3. Some accountants distinguish between a profit center and an *investment center*. They define an investment center as having control over capital investment in its business, whereas a profit center must take the plant and working capital it has and make the best of it. If it's helpful to make such a distinction in any company, it may be used. Generally, there is little need for the distinction because the origin, approval, and execution of investment plans for plant, product lines, and new businesses take place across levels of the company. If the investment center concept makes a difference in a particular company, it can usually be discerned by the use of measures of performance like *return on investment* or *return on capital*. When you see these measures used in addition to ordinary profit, you can be reasonably sure you're looking at an investment center.

Return on investment is either accrual basis net operating income or net cash flow (both are used), before interest and taxes (which are not caused by the business unit's primary activity), divided by operating assets employed.

Return on capital is either accrual basis net income or net cash flow, before taxes but after deducting interest, divided by the company's own resources (not borrowed) invested. If a separate balance sheet is prepared for the business unit, the denominator is merely the total of the capital section, or total assets minus total liabilities. Interest is deducted from income for return on capital because interest is a cost of the borrowed capital, and therefore a "result" of borrowing to reduce the company's own resources utilized. To make a ratio that reflects the company's results from its capital invested, both the borrowed capital and the income attributable to it (as represented by the interest paid for it) are taken out of the calculation.

It might seem that there should be a fourth kind of responsibility center, a *revenue center*, such as a sales department, but sales departments are generally viewed as cost centers with respect to their internal operational costs, and the revenue they produce is seen as their product. If this distinction seems too finely drawn, it need be no impediment to understanding and using accounting for total quality. Just change what needs changing for the ideas to fit into your organization and its style of operation.

CONTROLLABLE COSTS

Every operating entity has a *total cost* that includes all the costs of doing whatever it does. This includes *operating costs* such as material, labor, rent, utilities, and supervision. It also includes *financing costs* such as interest and costs of issuing and servicing stock. Finally, there are *allocated costs*. Some allocated costs might be operating costs, such as depreciation or plant maintenance. But some are corporate overhead, like corporate office charges.

As mentioned earlier, there is no point telling a manager about costs he can't do anything about. Of course, operating with a team concept, or using *open accounting* (covered in the next part of the book), you may wish to share all information with your management team, and even with workers. But when doing so, it's important to distinguish those costs that the individuals are being held responsible for from those they are merely informed about.

There are advantages to sharing full accounting information, as we will see later, but only with sufficient training to ensure the information is used advantageously. Even with minimal training, though, each manager can use information on those costs he can control.

Controllable costs are usually defined as those costs that a particular manager can authorize. Thus, he can avoid those costs by not authorizing them. That definition seems to be too restrictive, though, since there are costs that a manager, and even a worker, causes by his actions without explicitly authorizing. For example, a line worker can control indirect material by using more or less solvent or grease when cleaning his machine. He has no choice whether or not to clean it, and he certainly doesn't think of himself as granting authority to himself to use the material, but his decisions and methods of work determine the amount used.

You can see that controllable costs are usually those defined as direct costs or as production indirect in a production shop, or as direct costs and perhaps as supplies in an administrative department. Depending on the nature of a department's work, controllable costs may include quite a number of items, such as:

Travel
Direct Material
Training
Labor
Utilities
Supplies

In an administrative function, items such as utilities may be uncontrollable, but other items not listed above may be controllable, such as legal fees or bank charges.

Also, some controllable costs are not directly controllable, but arise from other decisions. For example, bank charges arise from the set of decisions about how to manage the company's cash and debt. They are not authorized in the direct sense of deciding "I think I'll buy $100 of banking today." Rather, they are a factor in making the less frequent, longer-term choices to set up accounts and loans in a particular way. These costs are nevertheless controllable costs to the treasury department, though not to other staff departments and certainly not to production departments.

In some cases, costs that don't seem controllable actually are. For instance, a preventive maintenance program that checks equipment on a calendar basis regardless of use may seem uncontrollable, but the amount of work required during the program is a result of the care given to the equipment as it is run. This is an example of a cost that may be unavoidable, in that it must be incurred at some level, but is controllable in that its amount is influenced by decisions made within an operating unit to which the cost is assigned.

Which costs are inherently controllable by a particular organizational unit depends upon the nature of its operation, which is the kind of controllability we have discussed so far. In addition, costs may be controllable because of the administrative policies of a company. For example, a new department may be organized and given space, desks, and equipment. It appears that the share of rent, depreciation, maintenance, and utilities are all uncontrollable by that department.

But suppose the department were organized using some of the total quality principles we discussed earlier. Suppose the members of the department were asked to team up and develop their own needs for space and equipment. In that case, the costs are controllable since they result from the organizational planning done by the work group itself. They may not be easy to change once they have been incurred, but they result from a decision of that department and should logically be reported so the decision makers can see the outcome of their choices.

The foregoing example brings us to the issue of *committed costs*. Committed costs are costs that can no longer be easily changed once incurred. Depreciation, when based on monthly or annual charges, is a committed cost. It should certainly be included in operating statements, but we are pretty much stuck with it. If we try to reduce it by getting rid of equipment, an accounting loss is recognized when the equipment is sold below original cost. (Of course, occasional gains also occur, and if another department can use the equipment, that's a plus.) Depreciation should be reported precisely because it raises these sorts of questions in the minds of operating managers and thereby improves the efficiency of capital equipment allocation in a business.

Sometimes allocated costs are also controllable costs. Where costs are allocated (absorbed, as covered earlier) on the basis of some direct input like labor, they may appear to be controllable through choices to use labor. But since the allocated costs are actually incurred independently of those choices, they are really not controllable costs at the level to which they are allocated. However, if costs are allocated on some other basis, one related to the purpose for which the cost is incurred, they may be said to be controllable in an organizational unit even though they are incurred in another unit. For example, if data processing costs are allocated to operating departments based on direct labor hours, the allocations are a result of the hours, but the costs actually incurred are not, and the cost is not a controllable cost. But if data processing costs are allocated based partly on number of employees (since paychecks and personnel records are kept on computers) and partly on number of reports prepared for the operating department, the data processing costs may be said to be controllable because the costs are actually incurred, at least in part, as a result of the decisions made in the operating department to employ people or to demand reports.

The whole set of issues surrounding committed costs, bases of allocation, and similar concepts deserves a separate discussion, so let's summarize before going on.

Controllable costs are those costs that an organizational unit can determine or influence by actions it takes. They include consumption of material and labor as well as less obvious costs like indirect material, travel, and maintenance. They also include some allocated costs when the allocation is based on a factor related to the use of the service whose cost is being allocated to a department. Controllable costs should always be reported to the manager who can influence them, since his managerial actions should be based on all pertinent information.

UNCONTROLLABLE COSTS

As we have just seen, some costs can be controlled, or at least influenced, by managers of operating units or staff departments. Other costs are beyond their control. But most companies report both controllable and uncontrollable costs to their managers. When they do, they must avoid the implication that every cost reported requires action. *Uncontrollable costs* should not be presented as though they were controllable. Such an implication will cause managers to waste time with matters that they can do nothing about.

Managers should be sufficiently well acquainted with the nature of cost behavior in their organizations and with the principles of engineering economy, economics, and accounting that they can distinguish between controllable and uncontrollable costs, but not all are adequately versed in such matters.

Managers often come up from production lines or functions such as marketing, sales, or maintenance. They must be trained in interpreting financial data. But even if they are not trained, their jobs can be simplified and their attention directed to productive ends if the reports they receive concentrate on controllable costs and either leave uncontrollable costs off entirely, or, better, include them for information but clearly indicate which costs are uncontrollable.

Costs that cannot be controlled are primarily general and administrative overhead allocations. But other costs may also be "given" to the manager of a department or shop. For example, a shop foreman probably has his equipment and space given to him, and he cannot change it no matter how much he may want to. Yet companies often report depreciation and space charges on department statements just as if they expect the manager to do something about them.

Even direct labor, thought to be the most controllable of costs, has a rigidity to it. Employees are often assigned to a department whether the supervisor wants them or not, as part of a "staffing plan" or as a training rotation for employees in certain development programs. Many companies also resist "short time" when work is slack, preferring to keep their skilled workers on staff and having them do useful work, but not directly productive in the "applied labor" sense that looks good on operating cost reports. Thus, even direct labor may be uncontrollable at low levels of unit activity for brief periods of time. As a partial solution, employees may clock "slack time" to indirect labor rather than directly to a job. If indirect labor is treated as an uncontrollable cost at the shop level, the remaining direct labor will properly represent work on product. It thereby once again becomes a controllable cost that reflects efficiency in producing the work unit's service or product.

So while we recognize that costs are never absolutely controllable and are influenceable only within a range, we nevertheless assign some costs as controllable and others as uncontrollable at different levels of the managerial pyramid.

The range within which costs may be controlled by a manager depends on the nature of the cost itself, decisions about the way the cost is determined (especially in the case of allocated costs), and the amount of discretion given the manager. Depreciation is an example of a cost that offers alternative treatments with respect to these criteria.

Depreciation is the allocation of the original cost of an item over the time that it is used. Things that last longer than one accounting period and that cost enough to be worth the trouble are *capitalized* and their cost is allocated to subsequent time periods through depreciation. Depreciation is therefore usually controllable only at the level where capital investment decisions are made, probably the plant level for some items and the strategic business unit or corporate level for high-dollar equipment or facilities. So this cost should be reported as controllable at the business unit level, but as uncontrollable at the shop level. At which intermediate level it becomes controllable depends on the capital purchase decision process at any particular company.

Depreciation also introduces another aspect of controllability: time. Some costs that can be controlled at the time of purchase become committed costs (discussed earlier) or *sunk costs* when the money is spent and the items purchased have been delivered. These costs are uncontrollable at the operating level, since the resources have been spent and cannot be recovered.

So does it make sense to report depreciation cost to a shop foreman? Many accountants and managers would say it does not make sense to give a manager information he can't use for direct action. Others would say that it does make sense if the amount is included in a section of the operating statement called "fixed costs," "uncontrollable costs," or perhaps "period costs." These terms have slightly different meanings to accounting technicians, but any of them will convey the meaning adequately to the intended audience. It also makes sense to report depreciation if it is based on machine hours rather than being a fixed monthly charge. In such a case, the efficiency of the shop in using its machines affects the amount charged to any job moving through it. As a reflection of machine usage, which the manager can affect, usage-based depreciation can be a controllable cost.

Chapter 5 will develop these ideas further in its discussion of direct costing and activity-based costing. Direct costing is a method of distinguishing costs on another theoretical basis, but it results in separating controllable from uncontrollable costs. Activity-based costing shows that apparently uncontrollable costs are actually a result of choices made in operating units; it reports that effect to them so they can make more economically valid resource decisions.

COST ALLOCATION AND TRANSFER PRICING

The preceding discussions of controllable and uncontrollable costs lead into another topic that will be treated at length in the next chapter on direct costing and activity-based costing. To prepare for those topics, though, a brief digression into arbitrary allocations and transfer pricing is warranted.

Cost Allocation

As we saw in the preceding material on cost accounting, most traditional accounting systems are absorption costing types. This means that the costs of the whole operation are allocated to the final products as much as is reasonably possible. For example, product support activities such as inspection, packing, tool room operation, plant maintenance, and utilities are allocated directly to units of output based on some direct input, such as direct labor hours or material dollars. As also described in the opening material, some period costs such as general and administrative are so remote from any unit of service or product that they are charged as period costs, and not allocated to the product. Selling costs are related to the sales reported for any period, so they are also included as period costs rather than being charged to the product.

The allocations that are made, though, are essentially arbitrary. They bear little relation to the use of these services in the production activities. For example, a shop with two large, computer-controlled machines has only one operator for both since they work virtually unattended once they are turned on and loaded with tools and material. Another shop has a dozen machine tools, each with its own operator. Based on direct labor hours, the shop with all the little machines gets twelve times the production indirect cost assignment. But the two huge machines actually take more electricity, management time, and such indirect time as production control labor than do the twelve little ones.

The opportunity for distorted cost accounting and erroneous managerial decisions is obvious as work is moved to the automated machine center, with its seemingly lower costs. Then costs go up because the support costs are higher. But no one knows why costs went up because costs are allocated on a basis unrelated to their actual causes.

Transfer Pricing

Transfer pricing is the assignment of a price to a unit of product as it moves from one profit center to another. Shops, plants, or subsidiaries "buy" products and services from others within a company, "paying" a transfer price. Using a transfer price allows each profit center to have a reasonable basis for determining a separate profit number.

The ideal transfer price is the market price for the same item or service. But if there is no established market for an intermediate product, as where the intermediate product is a subassembly, another basis must be found. Cost plus a percentage for overhead and profit is commonly used.

The U.S. tax laws have recently targeted transfer pricing as a problem since international companies used it as a way to move profits to favorable tax jurisdictions. If you encounter this situation, please recognize that it is a regulatory problem, not a theoretical accounting issue. The accounting theory is the same regardless of the tax law. A basic understanding of these topics is helpful in the development of direct costing and activity-based costing that follows.

5

INTRODUCTION TO DIRECT COSTING

DIRECT COSTING VERSUS INDIRECT COSTING

Direct costing is a cost accounting approach that has been around since the 1950s. Whenever it has been considered in opposition to absorption costing, it has won both the theoretical argument and the managerial argument. The basic idea of direct costing is that only *direct costs* should be assigned to a product. *Indirect costs* such as supervision, indirect material, or utilities (production indirect), and costs such as executive office operation, accounting, or finance (general and administrative or G&A) are not allocated to products. They are shown only in total rather than being broken down to a per-unit amount and added to product costs.

The only point on which absorption costing has been preferable is for financial accounting purposes. Absorption costing is preferred when the objective of an accounting statement is to see how revenue compares to cost of services rendered or items sold. Then the total cost of those items should be compared to the total revenue realized for them. The revenue is easy; it's the sales for the period covered by the report. Cost of goods sold or of services rendered is more difficult because there is a question of which costs of the business are costs of items sold and which are costs of just being in business.

Table 5-1 shows a standard income statement, prepared on an absorption costing basis. In it, all costs of the items or services sold are allocated to the products. Table 5-2 shows the same statement prepared on a direct costing basis. In this case, costs of indirect services and materials are separated and not allocated to the products. The difference in these statements is that indirect production costs are expensed in the period in which they are incurred, rather than being added to the cost of product.

You will note that these tables correspond to the principles in this chapter's first few paragraphs:

Table 5-1. Absorption Costing

	Dollars	Units	Per Unit
Sales	$2,138,000	1,638	$1,305
Cost of Sales:			
Beginning Inventory	$135,000	201	$672
Goods Manufactured			
Direct Material	$585,000		
Direct Labor	$302,000		
Production Indirect	$212,000		
Total Goods Manufactured	$1,099,000	1,675	$656
Goods Available for Sale	$1,234,000	1,876	$658
Less: Ending Inventory	($147,000)	(224)	$658
Gross Profit	$1,087,000	1,653	$636
	$1,051,000		
Selling Costs	$156,000		$94
General & Administrative Costs	$540,000		$327
Net Income before Income Taxes	$355,000		$215

Table 5-2. Direct Costing

	Dollars			Units	Per Unit
Sales			$2,138,000	1,638	$1,305
Cost of Sales:					
Beginning Inventory		$135,000		201	$540
Goods Manufactured					
Direct Material	$585,000				
Direct Labor	$302,000				
Total Goods Manufactured		$887,000		1,675	$530
Goods Available for Sale		$1,022,000		1,876	$545
Less: Ending Inventory		($147,000)	$875,000	(270)	$545
Contribution Margin			$1,263,000	1,606	$786
Production Indirect			$212,000		$132
Selling Costs			$156,000		$97
General & Administrative Costs			$540,000		$336
Net Income* before Income Taxes			$355,000		$221

*Net Income varies between absorption cost and direct cost statements because beginning inventory component of absorption cost statement includes production indirect costs of earlier periods, which may be different from those of the current period.

91

- In absorption costing, all production costs are assigned to products. Costs of products are recognized in the period when goods are sold or services are rendered. Only G&A and selling costs are expensed in the period when they are incurred. The costs of products include allocated costs such as supervision, depreciation, plant services, and sometimes staff functions such as personnel or even the cost of legal services for patents.
- In direct costing, only direct labor and material are assigned to products. Indirect costs incurred in the production process are recognized in the period in which they are incurred, just as G&A and selling costs are in absorption costing systems.

A compromise technique that can meet the requirements of generally accepted accounting principles (GAAP is what the auditors look for) and tax law, but still assist management in distinguishing controllable costs from uncontrollable costs is to prepare two sets of statements. First prepare internal statements on a direct costing basis for use by operating managers. Then allocate indirect costs to products for financial purposes separately, not on the statements given to production managers.

At this point, a digression is needed to explain the theoretical distinctions among fixed costs and variable costs, product costs and period costs, direct costs and indirect costs, or product-sustaining costs and capacity-sustaining costs and organization-sustaining costs. Although these terminology pairs are similar, they distinguish costs on slightly different theoretical bases.

The distinction between fixed and variable costs was covered at length earlier, in the discussion of cost-volume-profit analysis. In that discussion, it was demonstrated that the distinction between fixed and variable cost elements was necessary to determine optimum prices and output levels. To recapitulate, fixed costs are those that do not alter with changes in production volume, at least within the range of normal operations. Variable costs change more or less exactly with changes in production volume.

The distinction between product costs and period costs is slightly different. Product costs are incurred for the purpose of making an identifiable unit of output, while period costs are incurred in similar amounts each period, regardless of output.

Direct and indirect costs are similar to the terms above, but do differ somewhat, since some indirect costs vary with production volume. For example, indirect costs include supervision, which varies with volume when overtime requires the supervisory staff to work late with the workers. It also includes some items that are used in producing a service or item but are not directly applied to it, such as lubricants or rags and solvents. The use of these items varies more or less directly with production, but they are "shop indirect" costs. Even "plant indirect" costs may vary somewhat with production volume, such as maintenance or utilities.

Finally, we will look at the newer terms *product-sustaining*, *capacity-sustaining*, and *organization-sustaining* costs. Product-sustaining costs are the costs of actually developing and making the product. They include, of course, direct material and labor. They also include more remote costs such as design engineering and obtaining patents. In contrast, capacity-sustaining costs include the costs of having a plant to make the product in, including machinery, supervision, and maintenance. Organization-sustaining costs relate to simply being in business. These costs are chiefly G&A costs such as executive offices and their inhabitants, organization costs, most legal costs, annual audits, stockholder relations, finance, and portions of personnel and accounting.

Summary

In recent years, as total quality management has come along and workers from different functional areas have been able to consider a bigger picture, the emphasis has shifted from the overall financial statements dictated by GAAP to more action-oriented statements dictated by economic theory. Economic theory led to developing direct costing in the past, a practice whose time has come at last, and to activity-based costing (the next subject covered), as theoretically pure as a cost accounting system can be in a real situation.

INCREMENTAL COSTS

In every managerial accounting, finance, and engineering economy text there is a portion devoted to *relevant costs*. Although much space is taken up with the idea, it all comes down to a simple statement: for any management decision, the relevant costs are the costs that will be changed from one alternative to another.

The costs that will differ among alternatives are called by different names in different disciplines, but they are really synonyms. Accountants call them *incremental costs* or *differential costs*. Economists call them *marginal costs*.

We generally think of marginal costs as being variable costs, and so they are, but not always in the classic sense. If we are looking at a short-run production management decision to be made by a shop supervisor, the direct variable costs described previously, chiefly labor and material, are those that need to be considered (possibly with an added amount for employee benefits and shop supplies).

If the decision in view is somewhat longer-range in its impact, such as deciding whether to add capacity to the shop or to change the method of work by substituting equipment for labor, the cost of the equipment becomes a variable for the purposes of that decision, even though it would be a fixed cost for daily production decisions. Any amount saved by the new capability is also part of the marginal cost calculation. The net of amounts to be expended and amounts saved by any decision is the net relevant cost for that decision. It is the incremental cost or marginal cost, if you prefer those terms.

Some decisions are very long-range indeed, such as a decision to enter a whole new line of business. Such a decision requires consideration of administrative costs, plant costs, equipment costs, personnel costs, material costs, maintenance costs, and the entire "income statement full" of revenues and costs associated with the proposed line of business. In addition, such a large investment must be financed, and the financing costs such as stock registration or interest must be considered along with some return for risk and a reasonable profit.

CONTRIBUTION MARGIN

Although it sounds like the idea of marginal costs introduced in the last section, contribution margin is really a different idea. The idea of contribution margin has been discussed earlier under the topic of cost-volume-profit analysis (CVP) where it was the amount of revenue left over after covering the variable costs, as a contribution to fixed costs.

As often happens in accounting, the term *contribution margin* has more than one meaning. All the meanings stem from the same idea, that the contribution margin is the amount of revenue left after paying costs of providing the service or item sold. It is called contribution margin because it is the amount that each sale contributes to paying the overhead costs such as G&A and selling costs.

The first meaning is used in conventional financial accounting, where absorption costing principles are used for computing the cost of sales. In absorption costing, indirect production costs are included in the cost of the product, through cost allocations that have been previously illustrated. In the case of production of hard goods, the costs are ultimately transferred to inventory accounts until the items are sold, and the costs are then transferred to cost of sales on the income statement. The contribution margin in that meaning is the amount left over from revenue after reimbursing the inventory accounts for goods sold. In the case of services, the incurring of costs is usually simultaneous with the earning of revenue (no inventory) and the cost of sales is figured as costs are incurred, but indirect costs like supervision and equipment depreciation are still allocated to units of service. The contribution margin then is the amount available to cover such overhead costs as G&A and selling expenses.

The second meaning is used in direct costing, where contribution margin is the margin left from revenue after paying the direct costs of producing services or goods sold. In this case, the contribution margin will be higher because it must cover production indirect costs like supervision and equipment. Here, there may be considered to be two contribution margins, if you like: one might be called "contribution to production indirect costs" and the other might be the amount left after those costs have been subtracted and called "contribution to selling and general expenses."

REPORTING COSTS

The previous material on marginal costs and relevant costs has given an indication of which way we should go in choosing which costs to report to various levels of management. Since the only relevant costs for any managerial decision are the costs that will be changed by that decision, it follows that the only information that will produce useful action by any manager or worker is information on those costs that the person can affect. Information on costs that cannot be changed by any decision the manager might make should not be reported to him. So the question is, "What information can a manager act on to improve the company's performance?" The answer to that question takes us far from the apparently restrictive scope of reported information implied in the above paragraphs.

Of course, managers can affect the variable costs of the processes for which they are responsible. If I were the manager of an accounting department, my decisions about how fast to turn disbursements around, how many reviews should be made of payroll distributions, which processes to perform on computers and which to do manually, and whether to hire more workers or use overtime would all affect the costs of my department. Therefore, I should receive reports that show these costs.

As the manager of an accounting department, I cannot affect the utilities used (the lights will be on anyway), the rent paid, the executive salaries, or the costs of operating the purchasing, maintenance, and personnel departments, even though I use their services. Therefore, it appears those costs should not be reported to me.

But not so fast! I do indeed affect the costs of operating the departments whose services I use. User departments do not control the internal operations of service departments directly by selecting operating methods and resources, the way they control their own operations. User departments do affect the overall costs of service departments, though, by determining the amount of service demanded, thereby setting the amount of variable costs to be incurred. In the longer term, demand levels over an extended time also determine the size of the service departments and thus the size of the building needed and similar fixed costs. Remember that the term "fixed costs" is situationally dependent on the level of management and the time period. Any cost is variable by the right person given enough time.

So now there is a new category of costs to show along with the variable costs of my own department. I should also know the per-unit variable costs of service departments I use so that I can make rational choices about using their services and thereby reduce overall company costs.

This opens a whole new set of questions: "Cost per unit of what? What is a unit of personnel service or travel planning service? If I know the variable costs of services I use, am I to be judged on those costs too, or are they just for information? If they're just for information, why should I care what goes on in someone else's department as long as I get the service I need for free?"

The need to answer these questions led to a further development in cost accounting, namely *activity-based costing* (ABC). ABC will be covered in the next few sections. For now, though, it's enough to recognize that any cost he can affect should be reported to a manager. Only by knowing what his costs are can he act to optimize the mix of resources used in achieving his production goals.

We mentioned that there are costs peculiar to departments that the department manager cannot affect, at least by his own action in the short term. Such costs include depreciation, utilities, and plant services. These are more or less fixed costs whose amount was determined earlier by those who selected the plant and equipment to be bought. Should they be reported to an operating manager? The opening discussion suggests that since they are not relevant to his daily supervisory tasks, they are not useful to him. But might his knowledge of fixed costs be useful to the company?

Such knowledge might indeed be useful to the company, because the manager is usually not limited to decisions in the short term. Remembering that all costs are variable at the right level of management and at the right time, we see that these seemingly fixed costs can be changed. The question is whether they can be changed by a particular manager who receives a particular report of costs. Often, the answer is that when a fixed cost is "up for renewal," that is, when replacement or similar decisions are to be made, the operating manager is consulted. An operating manager who regularly sees the depreciation and maintenance costs of his equipment is better equipped to assist in replacement choices.

So now it appears that an operating manager should have his department's variable costs reported to him because he affects them in his daily decisions.

He should have the per-unit variable costs of services he uses reported to him because he affects the total cost of operating the company through his demand for internal services. He should have the fixed costs of his own department reported to him because he is usually called on to participate when these costs cease to be fixed, as in replacement decisions and process design decisions within his own department.

This discussion has now come full circle, leading to reporting costs that managers affect only indirectly through service demand or only occasionally through capital investment or process design. The opportunity for operating managers to misunderstand the meaning of their cost reports is significant. They are apt to look for ways to respond to the information. Response to information about activities not under their direct daily control is likely to lead to wasted effort and misdirected attention.

The way out of this cycle is training. Just as total quality management requires that each worker and manager learn the principles of TQM to act in accordance with them and in harmony with one another, total quality accounting requires that each worker and manager learn the principles of economics and of cost accounting that give rise to the information reported to him or her. When they learn how to interpret and use the information, it can be used correctly and can benefit the company.

DIRECT AND PRODUCT COSTING

We have seen that direct costing is superior to absorption costing for managerial decision-making because it does not disguise fixed costs among the variable costs when computing product costs. We have not, however, discussed how product costs can be computed under direct costing.

With absorption costing, production indirect costs are included in product costs by allocating them to products as they move through production cost centers. Direct costs such as direct labor and direct material are assigned to production lots or to service projects as the direct costs are incurred and paid. Indirect costs such as supervision and facility costs are totalled and moved from expense accounts to work-in-process accounts (and later from work-in-process to inventory or directly to cost of sales). The amount of the total indirect cost to be added to each production lot, job, or project is computed by using some allocation base like direct labor hours or direct material dollars. The proportion that the total allocation base bears to the amount used by each lot is the proportion of total indirect costs assigned to the lot. This is usually figured as an amount per unit of allocation base, such as $5 per direct labor hour. The difference in production cost per unit calculated by absorption costing methods and that calculated by direct costing is the amount of indirect cost allocated to the products in the absorption costing model.

If we are to calculate transfer prices that will cover our full costs of operation, though, or to value inventories under the IRS rules, we must include these indirect costs in our total product cost, even though they are misleading for managerial purposes.

The question is, how do we calculate a fully allocated absorption cost needed for some purposes from a more theoretically useful direct costing statement? The answer may be obvious to some, but for most of us it takes considerable thought, particularly if we have spent years learning how to perfect absorption costing methods and reports. It is that we allocate indirect costs, but we allocate them afterwards, on the bottom of the direct costing statement. This also allows us to see the portion, if any, that may be unallocated or overallocated if standard rates are used and if they differ from the proportional amounts that would have been used without standard rates.

Another advantage of this presentation is that it can be refined to separate fixed costs from variable costs for even more thorough managerial analysis. Further, the variable and fixed costs can be kept separate through the reporting process, so downstream managers who use the department's product can make rational decisions about which costs will be saved or incurred if they vary their demand for the products.

To summarize:

1. Direct costing is preferable for management because it separates direct from indirect and, if constructed to do so, from fixed costs. It thereby allows managers to make rational economic choices because the data corresponds to the fixed and variable components that economic theory requires. Decisions that can be made more rationally include:

a) Make-or-buy;
b) Product line continuance;
c) Territory continuance;
d) Automation of processes;
e) Alternate production processes or routings.

They can be made more rationally because the costs that will change with the decision being considered can be separated from the costs that will stay the same, so the principle of incremental or marginal costs can be applied.

2. Direct costing is preferable for management because it points up those costs that are managed by changing production methods, those that are managed by changing production capacity, and those that are managed by chang-

ing organizational patterns. Thus management's attention is focused on effective cost control possibilities more quickly.

3. Direct costing is compatible with certain regulatory and investor-inspired requirements for fully absorbed costs to be assigned to products, but the assignment of indirect and fixed costs is made after the direct costs have been assigned and the other costs have been identified in total. This way, rational management is possible and fully allocated costs are also available.

ACTIVITY-BASED COSTING

Absorption costing, the conventional method for both internal management and external reporting, attempts to assign all production costs to final products or services. Some costs can be assigned directly to processes, jobs, or projects and where individual units are large enough to justify separate accounting for each one, costs can be assigned to distinct units, as in construction or aircraft.

Other costs are harder to trace to separate units of production or service. These include indirect costs such as supervision, rent, and utilities. Other kinds of costs that are hard to trace to units of final product or service are general and administrative costs. These costs are usually thought of as the costs of being in business rather than assigned to any particular unit of production, or to production effort at all. They include executive offices, administrative departments, and research departments. Such costs are usually not allocated to products but instead are subtracted from revenue each month to determine net income.

One long-standing argument against such conventional costing has been that cost allocations are more or less arbitrary; they do not necessarily represent the degree to which different products actually cause indirect costs to be incurred. Another criticism is that indirect costs tend to be fixed costs, at least in the immediate time period and with respect to the management level receiving itemized reports of such costs. The implication that indirect costs are related solely to production volume is misleading. It can cause economically incorrect choices by line managers.

The preceding portion of the chapter has shown that an answer to these criticisms is direct costing. Direct costing attempts no cost allocations. Instead, it recognizes that indirect costs are not cause by any particular unit of production, but are often incurred regardless of production levels. We saw that a compromise is sometimes used where generally accepted accounting principles (GAAP) or IRS regulations require assigning indirect costs to products kept in inventory. Here, direct costing is sometimes used for internal management reports but absorption costing principles are applied and allocations are made for regulatory purposes at the bottom of the report or even omitted from the report entirely and simply made in the financial accounting records.

Thus, direct costing is preferable to absorption costing for line management purposes, but still does not address the issue that led to its invention—absorption cost allocations assign costs to products without clear causal links. Direct costing merely stops making allocations. Really accurate cost assignment models require that costs are assigned to the cost objects (products, jobs, or departments) that benefit from them.

An answer to this problem was developed at about the same time that total quality management began to attract attention in the United States, and was partly caused by TQM demands. Whether TQM caused *activity-based costing* (ABC) to be developed is uncertain because they were adopted together in some places and separately in others. Today, ABC is often used as a decision tool even where TQM is not formally adopted. In any event, ABC is certainly a part of the TQM tool kit and can be helpful wherever the TQM effort leads to questions about products' or services' *true costs*.

Activity-based costing begins with the principle that all costs are incurred to benefit some customer. That customer may be a customer of the company's final products or an intermediate process or a capacity-related or organization-sustaining cost object. Whatever the beneficiary of a cost, there is always some objective in its incurrence, and the cost should be traced and assigned to the beneficiary.

Activity-based costing recognizes, in the same way as absorption and direct costing, that some items are applied directly to end products. Therefore, it assigns the costs of direct labor and direct material to products, services, projects, or jobs just as absorption and direct costing do.

Other costs are production indirect costs. Absorption costing allocated these costs to products according to some algorithm, such as direct labor hours or direct material dollars. Direct costing did not allocate them at all. But activity-based costing recognizes that products and internal departments benefit from costs that are traditionally viewed as indirect, and attempts to trace these costs to the benefiting units. Activity-based costing further extends its tracing efforts to include costs that are traditionally classified as general and administrative wherever causal or beneficial links can be established between a cost and some product or organizational unit.

Thus, the cost objects, the things whose costs we wish to know, are products or internal organizational units, just as in absorption and direct costing. The cost elements to be assigned are also such things as labor, material, supervision, rent, and service department operations. The new feature that makes activity-based costing different is the attempt to trace these costs and assign them according to measurable benefits, rather than allocating them arbitrarily using an allocation base that does not, except by chance, reflect the degree to which the ultimate cost object actually caused or benefitted from the source cost elements.

Activities as Intermediate Cost Objects

Activity-based costing assigns direct costs to cost objects in the same way that conventional costing methods do. Its treatment of indirect costs is different, however. It assigns costs that would have been classed as indirect costs, wherever possible, as direct costs of intermediate cost objects. These intermediate cost objects are the activities carried on within departments that benefit a product or another department.

For example, personnel departments process a few personnel actions for their own people, but their real purpose and most of their work is for others in the company. Some internal service activities might be those shown in Table 5-3.

Activity-based costing assigns costs to these activities as cost objects, then further assigns the costs of the activities to the benefiting products or units. Recently, industrial engineers and production managers have begun to use the scheme shown in Table 5–4 to classify the costs of activities. This scheme is not necessary to ABC but can be helpful in thinking about possible cost objects and the cost elements that might be traced to them for further assignment based on activity measures.

By assigning costs through measures of the amount of resource-consuming activity that benefits a particular organizational unit, we can find the total

Table 5-3. Activities by Department

Personnel	Accounting and Finance	Engineering	Maintenance
Hiring	Reporting	Preparing Process Specification	Repairing Equipment
Promotion	Payroll	Issuing Engineering Changes	Performing Scheduled Maintenance
Pay Change	Capital Investment Analysis	Capital Investment Analysis	Cleaning Work Areas
Annual Review	Disbursements	New Product Design	Moving Equipment
Benefits Change	Drawing on Line of Credit	Developing Training	Installing Equipment
Conducting Training	Preparing Stock Issue		

Table 5-4. Examples of Cost Classifications

Direct Product Costs	Product-sustaining	Capacity-sustaining	Organization-sustaining
Direct Labor	Design	Maintenance	Debt Service
Direct Material	Engineering Changes	Equipment Charges	Executive Offices
	Specific Tools and Dies	Production Supervision	Licenses and Taxes
		Assigned to	
Internal Service Departments, Projects, Jobs Directly as Performed	Products and Product Groups over Life Cycle through Activity Measures	Internal Service Departments, Projects, Jobs through Activity Measures	Not Reassigned; Treated as Period Costs

cost of operating that unit, including the cost of any internal services it uses. The cost of internal services will be the total cost of producing the services (the activities) and will reveal to each manager just what costs he causes in other departments. An activity-based cost statement for both the department and for the product can help.

We must answer some pertinent questions before we can produce such a statement, though. They are:

1. What activities are carried out?
2. What resources are used in those activities?
3. What are the outputs of those activities?
4. How much does each unit of output cost?
5. Who uses or benefits from the outputs?
6. How many output units are used by each customer?

Setting Up an Activity-Based Model

These questions lead directly into the steps needed to establish an activity cost model of a business and to calculate the activity costs that apply to each internal user of services and to each ultimate product. The steps are listed differently by different practitioners and are not necessarily carried out in the same order. Some can even be performed concurrently; for example, once activities are defined and listed, their costs can be collected by one team while another traces their beneficiaries. These two efforts come together when it is time to assign activity costs to beneficiaries.

Another variation on these steps relies on the notion that it is possible to begin with a department and define its activities, then trace its outputs to beneficiaries. It is also possible to begin with a department or product and trace backward to the activities whose outputs they use. For a pilot ABC project, where part of a business unit rather than a whole self-contained business unit is being costed, tracing downstream will distribute pilot departments' costs. However, unless downstream departments use only outputs of pilot departments, there will be no place where a full set of activity costs is collected for any beneficiary. Thus, unless a comprehensive activity costing project is being conducted, upstream tracing of costs from beneficiary to provider is the only workable choice.

Accepting the risk of disagreement about the number of steps and their order, the steps are:

1. Define units or products for which activity costs are to be calculated.
2. Determine the activities that are conducted within those units or for those products.
3. Classify the costs of these activities as
   a) direct labor and benefits;
   b) direct material;
   c) indirect costs.
4. Trace resources used in providing direct labor and material (such as hiring, training, and paying personnel or purchasing, moving, and storing material).
5. Trace indirect cost elements.
6. Determine the cost of each resource, including all of its supporting cost elements, such as those listed in step 4.
7. Establish causal relationships between activities within the target cost object (organizational unit or product) and activities that provide resources to the target cost object.
8. Select activity measures that relate the amount of activity in supplier organizational units to the outputs that are passed to beneficiaries. For example, for the payroll activity the number of checks might be used. We might select the number of material moves for the material-handling activity cost assignment, or we might select total weight moved. Activity measures that fit each company will be highly dependent on the details of its internal processes.

9. Use activity measures to assign activity costs to benefiting organizational units or products.

When carrying out these steps in practice, cross-assignments sometimes become necessary, as for example, when management information services (MIS) serves the accounting department with programming and data processing, while accounting serves the MIS department with payroll and cost reporting services.

Another complication that arises when tracing costs upstream is that it leads to calculating activity costs for all supporting activities as though they were also targets of the pilot project. Thus, pilot activity costing projects are disproportionately expensive. The upside is that if the pilot is expanded, much of the work is already done.

The effort required to cut across conventional cost accounting classifications and to gather costs on the new basis of activities, rather than departments or ultimate products, is great enough that activity costing, while quite revealing of the actual costs of providing internal services or of making products and services for final customers, should be undertaken either with a view to evaluating it for company-wide adoption or to conducting only rare analyses. Regularly producing two separate sets of cost statements is probably too expensive to be a real option.

Conclusion

Activity-based costing is a powerful tool for total quality companies in its ability to identify the costs actually caused by each downstream activity, department, and product. It accords with the principles of TQM in its customer focus and in its data-based approach to cost assignment. If implemented in a participatory way, it can be accepted by line managers. Finally, ABC facilitates such total quality practices as process value analysis and benchmarking. It merits serious consideration as a TQM tool wherever line managers require complete, comprehensive cost information.

PART III

INTEGRATING TQM AND COST ACCOUNTING TO SERVE INTERNAL AND EXTERNAL CUSTOMERS

When we started exploring total quality management and cost accounting, we noted that each of us comes to the subject with a different state of current knowledge. Some readers are total quality experts but are not comfortable with their expertise in accounting. Others are skilled accountants, but feel unsure about what TQM is and how it's done. A third group of readers may be uncertain about both subjects and, finally, some are informed about both areas, but are unsure how to integrate them.

Readers who feel sure of their knowledge in one area or the other may have skipped one of the earlier sections of the book. Some may even have skipped both parts, beginning here.

In this part of the book, we will look at the kinds of questions that managers ask of accounting. We will see how such questions can be answered in ways that line managers can understand, because line managers participate in developing their own answers. The degree of accounting training for operating managers will be considered, as will the degree of operational understanding that any company may wish to provide for its accountants.

We will also examine some adaptations of TQM methods from their beginnings in manufacturing processes to their uses in improving accounting products and processes. Such methods can be used, and are being used today in a few pioneering companies, to make accounting functions work better internally and to produce outputs that are more useful to the company's internal customers.

The practical techniques that are effective in TQM implementations are not peculiar to TQM. It is a formal structure for enlisting the whole organization and a commitment to using these techniques for continuous improvement that distinguish TQM from a hodgepodge of fashionable fads. Also, despite what followers of one or another TQM guru might say, there is no one technique that by itself makes an effort a TQM effort. Each company can choose those tools that are best for its own situation.

INTEGRATION

There have been few truly new accounting principles since accounting was invented at the end of the fifteenth century. One theme of Part 2 was that the principles are sometimes forgotten or distorted, but they're not brand-new and haven't changed in at least 50 years; only our ability to manipulate transaction data has changed. So while we have new accounting capabilities, they are mostly applications of old principles through new techniques.

These fundamental accounting principles are derived from the science of economics. In turn, principles of economics are embedded in human nature, which hasn't changed in history. We have developed industrial cost accounting so we can use these economic principles in choosing among alternative actions. So while there are occasional innovations, they are rare. Most opportunities to improve accounting products and processes lie in applying established principles to new situations using new data-handling capability.

These fundamentals are the "gold" that we are mining as we examine the possibilities offered by TQM and by modern accounting techniques. In addition, some new possibilities have been described in preceding sections. The most revolutionary is the new data-handling capabilities of the computer. At the end of this part, some future directions are covered to complete the picture.

In reviewing these tools for integrating modern accounting options and total quality management, many readers will recognize concepts that they have seen before, but under other names. They will also see concepts that they have been vaguely aware of, concepts that follow from ideas that are basic to economics, industrial engineering, finance, or other disciplines, but that have not been articulated before in a context combining operations and accounting capabilities.

TERMINOLOGY

A minor difficulty arises from the fact that we all come to the subject from different directions and that we are accustomed to different terms. Readers who have dealt with the issues covered in the earlier parts of the book are aware that many terms correspond to those they are familiar with, while others seem foreign. This happens because some terms are imported from operations, some from engineering, some from finance, and some from accounting. Terminology is not settled in either the TQM arena or in many of the new accounting approaches. While the "most common" terms have been sought for this book, competition is still going on in the "marketplace of ideas."

Each reader should take what looks most useful in his own situation, apply the terms that are most comfortable to him and to his "customers," and bypass the ideas that may not be quite as good in any particular organization.

CONCLUSION

To sum up, then, the purpose of this part of the book is to correct the deficiencies that seem to exist in TQM and in accounting:

1. Although TQM has much to offer accounting practitioners as part of the business team, such practitioners have not used it fully to provide value to their customers.
2. The other members of the business team, even at nominally total quality organizations, have not included their accountants as full partners and have not benefitted from the capabilities of modern accounting tools.

So let's see how to produce total quality accounting products using total quality processes. Let's see how to use accounting products to help produce a total quality organization.

6

THE COST OF QUALITY

If your company is beginning its total quality management effort, one of the first tasks given to the accounting department is to calculate the *cost of quality*. From the discussions in the first parts of the book, readers may have gathered that operating managers often distrust accounting and don't always see accountants as useful members of operations teams. The Institute of Management Accountants' study *Management Accounting in the New Manufacturing Environment* reveals that operating managers are dissatisfied with the information they receive. Operating managers do, however, have confidence in the objectivity of their organizations' accounting functions. It's just that they believe that conventional cost allocation schemes and cost assignments do not correspond to operating realities.

Consequently, although traditional accounting models are not fully trusted by others in most organizations, the accountants themselves are. So the controller's department is likely to get the assignment of calculating a value for the *cost of quality*. Philip B. Crosby, whose seminal book *Quality is Free* has been mentioned earlier, even recommends giving accountants this assignment, because of their integrity and the trust they have earned as objective score-keepers.

An obstacle to carrying out a cost of quality determination is that the cost of quality concept is not well defined, and there is no clear agreement among practitioners as to what should be included or how it should be assigned dollar amounts.

WHAT IS THE COST OF QUALITY?

Some practitioners view cost of quality as having two components, prevention costs and failure costs. The first of these, *prevention costs*, includes all costs of quality assurance efforts. These include inspection, statistical process control, shelf-life programs to prevent spoilage, and the like. Any cost that is incurred to detect incipient failure of a physical product or to ensure the acceptability and effectiveness of a service is a prevention cost. Prevention costs also include quality control measures to keep incipient failures from developing at all, such as design reviews, vendor certification programs, and quality orientation training. Prevention keeps customers from becoming dissatisfied with the goods and services they receive from the organization.

Prevention costs are also incurred in the production of intermediate products such as parts and subassemblies, and in earlier phases of product design and of service or project planning. The now accepted practice of forming design teams that include suppliers with production or operating personnel ensures that failures of the ultimate product are prevented even before the product goes into prototype production.

A second class of cost of quality elements is the *cost of failure*. These costs are the costs of making a bad product that does not perform as required in the customers' hands, or of performing services that do not meet the customers' requirements. Such costs include in-field repair, warranty, scrap, and rework. All such costs are incurred because some process created an output that did not meet specifications.

A formal distinction is sometimes made within this category of "cost of failure" between the costs of internal failure and the costs of external failure. Costs of internal failure are costs of performance defects discovered before an item is passed on to a customer. It includes scrap and rework costs. Costs of external failure are costs of correcting things for the customer who has not received what was required. These costs include warranty costs and in-field service, as well as any price adjustments or other accommodations that must be made to satisfy customers in such cases.

Some practitioners would consider a third kind of cost of quality—*cost of assessment* (also called *appraisal costs*). Costs of assessment include all elements that allow the organization to determine the level of quality that is being produced. Those who use it distinguish it from cost of prevention and cost of failure in that it is not as action-oriented as the other classes of cost of quality, but merely constitutes a report card. Those who make this distinction would include inspection costs, supplier surveillance, and prototype evaluation as a separate category. Those who do not make this distinction consider such costs as prevention costs.

Another cost of quality (or more accurately, of poor quality) relating to customer behavior is sometimes mentioned in TQM implementations but is seldom pursued. It is the *opportunity cost of sales lost* because of customers' poor experience or because of poor reputation in the market. It's easy to see why this aspect is seldom addressed directly, since no one can tell precisely how much customers might have bought if quality had been better. Even harder is an appraisal of lost revenue that results from accepting lower prices than might have been commanded in the marketplace by a premium product or service.

To estimate the cost of lost revenue from lost volume or from lower pricing requires trusting the marketing department, a source that is alien to most accountants. Such data is based on estimates and conclusions that accountants often find hard to swallow because they are based on "might-have-beens" rather than on past events that are observable and measurable in objective ways.

Calculating the value of lost sales is exceedingly difficult and involves a number of factors:

1. The lost gross profit under conventional absorption accounting.
2. The lost gross profit based on marginal cost under direct costing, which is more in keeping with economic theory as long as the company is operating below capacity.
3. The lost benefit of added market share in improving profitability across all sales, including those being made to current customers.
4. The value of added volume in moving the company further along the "experience curve" (a principle that is of real value when reducing costs over time, and that lies behind the striving for market share).

The preceding considerations illustrate the difficulty of producing cost of quality figures that will satisfy the accountant's typical preference for "accuracy," which we usually interpret to mean that a figure is based on objectively measured counts and historical values. Despite the difficulties, a new total quality organization will probably insist on some estimate of the cost of quality, and will almost certainly require the accounting department to produce it.

This cost of quality appraisal is likely to be the accountants' first opportunity to join the TQM effort, and should not be avoided by the accounting department. Rather, it should be accepted gladly, and even eagerly sought, since it allows the accounting department to be part of the company's main effort. Similarly, management should not ask any other department to perform this task, since accounting will have most of the relevant data and will understand its sources and legitimate interpretations. The accounting department is also likely to be accepted by others in the organization as an objective judge of cost information.

With team members from industrial engineering, operations, and quality assurance departments, the accounting function can make one of the first significant steps in any TQM implementation.

HOW CAN THE COST OF QUALITY BE CALCULATED?

When beginning a TQM effort, a company will probably ask for a cost of quality calculation right away, as a way of seeing what the potential benefits will be if quality is improved. Unfortunately, the established accounting system's ledgers will probably not yield cost elements that make up the cost of quality. Instead, cost of quality will be mixed in with the general operating costs of the business. Later, it is likely that the accounting system will be redesigned to allow collection of such costs routinely.

Internal Failures

Some changes that will be needed in handling cost of quality within a company's normal accounting procedures are in the treatment of scrap and rework costs. In many companies, the cost of scrap is not collected, but the cost of producing a whole job or project is reported all together. Direct material and labor are added to allocated indirect costs to yield total job cost. When the job consists of many parts or products, rather than a single item like a building, it is then divided by the total output, and a cost per unit results. Any mistakes or scrap parts are merely thrown out, and their cost becomes part of the cost of the whole job, and thereby part of the cost of good units.

Similarly, where rework is performed in the shop that makes a faulty product, that cost is also often buried in the cost of all of the product. Where items must be sent back to an earlier step, the cost of moving, setup, and scheduling may be included in total job cost or even in indirect costs that are allocated to all jobs.

If a company is doing its cost accounting this way, it has no convenient way of capturing the past cost of quality failure, but must estimate through engineering studies. A change to separately state the costs of items scrapped and the cost of rework effort must be made in the accounting system for the future, though. Such a change can readily be made by creating a cost account within each job to which the accumulated production cost of scrapped items is transferred at the stage of production where the scrap occurs. Thus, items scrapped near the end of their processing cost more than those scrapped early. Rework costs can also be entered in a separate account in each job, rather than being added to the existing basic labor, setup, or material cost accounts of the job.

There is some controversy over whether rework and scrap costs should be "fully burdened" with indirect costs assigned to a job, or should be direct costs only. The argument for direct costs is that only the direct costs are actually caused by the rework or extra items made to allow for scrap. Indirect costs are typically fixed costs that would be incurred anyway.

The argument for using "fully burdened" costs is that the fixed costs result from the basic size of the production facility, equipment, and organization, and they were sized to accommodate a production planning outlook that included scrap and rework, so the fixed costs are in fact caused by the scrapped items and by the effort required to deal with scrap and rework.

Of these choices, it seems best to use whatever method is used for costing good product, either full absorption costing or direct costing. This will be more credible to those who are accustomed to the present reporting mode of an organization and will facilitate comparisons. If the choice is a new one, the "fully burdened" choice seems better for giving an initial appraisal of what the company's costs would have been if it had been a total quality organization from the beginning, but the "direct cost" choice might be better if the facility is taken as a given that cannot be changed. Each company must make its own decision based on the management methods prevalent there.

External Failures

In looking at external failure costs, warranty costs are often collected and reported separately by companies. But sales returns and allowances are not often separated as to cause. Thus, a company can't always tell whether its returns and allowances or other price adjustments given to customers are due to quality failures or to other causes such as competitive factors in the marketplace. The accounting system should segregate returns for quality problems from those having other causes.

In similar fashion, in-field service should be separated into warranty, repair, and other categories that may be useful in appraising cost of quality. Warranty costs incurred within a production facility, where goods are returned for repair, should also be separately stated. Warranty costs can be figured using either direct costs or full absorption costs as seems to best fit the company's situations of operating near capacity and of using one or another method in normal reporting (discussed above).

Finally, the cost of customer "hotlines" and customer service departments cannot be overlooked as costs of correcting failures where a product or service does not meet a customer's requirements. Even where the customer appears to be at fault, it may be that the instructions or marking on a product are not as good as needed for trouble-free operation in the hands of a customer. Such instructions and markings are also part of the product, and if they don't work for the customer, a quality failure has occurred.

Failure Prevention

Now that we've covered the cost of lost sales and the costs of failure, let's discuss the cost of prevention. As noted, costs of prevention may be considered to include all costs of actions taken to ensure products and services are produced correctly to meet customers' requirements. Such costs may include costs of design reviews, quality control plans, vendor certification, process capability studies, inspection and test equipment, preventive maintenance of production equipment, and training operating personnel in both job skills and quality methods.

It is usually thought that prevention is cheaper than correction after bad product is made, or worse, after customers are disappointed. Such conclusions must be taken on faith in many cases, though. Although most TQM consultants would have us believe it that way, as an article of faith, their own statistical methods contradict it. Recall that in statistical process control charting, when setting the number of standard deviations from the mean that trigger an investigation for special causes, the decision depends on the cost of looking for a special cause when none actually exists compared to the cost of ignoring one that does exist. These costs multiplied by the probability of each event occurring determine the number of standard deviations that are used in setting limits beyond which a measurement will trigger an investigation.

Since even the most rigorous statistical control proponents recognize that costs must be balanced in making quality decisions, the investment in prevention has to be weighed against the cost of resulting failures. Fortunately for quality advocates, many of the activities classed as prevention-oriented in the cost of quality calculation are also needed to operate the business even without a TQM implementation. Job training, preventive maintenance, and like costs must be incurred in any case, so it makes sense to do them right, reducing quality failures later.

It can be difficult to determine whether the costs of certain activities such as training or preventive maintenance, which have traditionally been classed as production indirect or general and administrative costs, ought to continue their traditional treatment on the theory that they are really just the lowest-cost way to conduct production functions, or whether they ought to be classed as costs of quality. There are a number of possible answers. One is to divide the costs between the two cost categories. Another is to compare the costs of such elements before the TQM effort to those after, and ascribe the change to TQM; a drawback is that the request for cost of quality information usually precedes the TQM implementation. Another is to continue the traditional practice for most reporting purposes, but to make a separate cost of quality calculation when it is requested. Under this alternative, the same costs might be included in both production indirect and quality costs, depending on the purpose of the initial inquiry.

USING AN ACTION TEAM TO CALCULATE THE COST OF QUALITY

Cases where cost of quality is hard to define are excellent opportunities to bring the methods of TQM to bear on the TQM implementation process itself. All affected parties can be appointed to an action team. The team can include accountants, of course, but also quality assurance, operations, process design, and product design representatives.

The advantages of using such a team include acceptability of results, added insight, training and awareness for the team members, and an early opportunity to break down barriers to cooperation and communication in the total quality organization. Like all early attempts at a new way of doing business, team members must be carefully chosen. The participants in a *cost of quality action team* will probably become quality leaders in their parent departments, at least until the rest of the department has caught up during later phases of the TQM implementation process. Therefore, they should be willing, capable, and respected in their parent departments.

CONCLUSION

To summarize, cost of quality is a fundamental concept in most total quality management efforts, and calculating it is one of the first things to be done. It is a chance for the accounting function to join in the effort at the beginning. Since there are many factors to consider, and some ambiguities, an action team can be a good way to get the required information on cost of quality while also getting total quality practices started.

7

IMPLEMENTING TOTAL QUALITY MANAGEMENT— USING EXISTING ORGANIZATIONAL PATTERNS

RECOGNIZING ORGANIZATIONAL UNIQUENESS

Every company is different in many ways. Each has an existing culture, informal relationships, a formal organization, products, and customer groups. No organization is quite like another, even in the Army. Just as each company differs from every other, parts of a company differ from one another. The approach that works well in one area may need some adaptation to work in another. To provide total quality accounting for an organization requires that when total quality is made part of the accounting functions, its techniques are adapted to the accounting department's needs and culture.

The following features may be incorporated in an accounting department's TQM implementation:

1. A dedicated accounting TQM leader, either a consultant or a trained member of the existing employee group. One of each might be best in many instances.
2. Training in TQM methods for accountants.
3. Training in the whole organization's TQM objectives, especially the objectives of accounting's main customer groups.
4. Training in modern cost accounting alternatives and economic theory, so need-specific accounting products can be crafted when required.
5. Formation of cross-functional groups to meet regularly for the purpose of finding improvement opportunities in accounting products.

6. Formation of groups within the accounting function to meet regularly for the purpose of finding improvement opportunities in accounting processes.

HIRING CONSULTANTS

These changes in behavior for most companies are fundamental; consequently, assistance from the outside will probably be needed to ensure results and to guard against pursuing unproductive avenues. The first part of this book suggests that a consultant be used in most total quality management implementations. Such a consultant should be carefully chosen. While many are effective and helpful, none is likely to achieve maximum results by applying a canned "solution" to every situation. Therefore, a company should expect to spend some time finding a consultant who fits its needs, one who will take the necessary time and effort to develop a tailored implementation process together with company officials and workers. TQM is such a revolution in most companies that time must be taken to bring all affected groups aboard, especially worker groups and professional groups like unions, the legal department, engineering, and finance.

A general consulting firm can be selected if it includes TQM specialists. Such a firm will have the added advantage of access to additional specialists in personnel, production, accounting, and other disciplines. For an implementation that is to span the whole company, a member of the consulting team must be knowledgeable about administrative processes. It too often happens that staff processes are left behind in the rush to get operations functions "TQMed." A counterweight to the diverse capabilities of large consulting firms is that too often each client gets "cookie cutter" service, where each consulting engagement is forced to be as much like the last one as possible, so the firm can deliver on its contract and move on, rather than fitting the service to the client's organization. There are many fine individuals in both large practices and solo practices, and at every sized firm in between. The personal fit probably matters more than the name.

Another consideration in choosing a consultant is that TQM will take a long time to become part of most companies' cultures because it's such a radical change. Therefore, it may be a good idea to engage a consultant in administrative and financial TQM aspects as well as an operations expert and a statistician.

Whatever choice an organization makes about seeking assistance from outside, it is essential that all such helpers work in concert with one another and with the company's personnel. A plan for implementing TQM in a company will require time, work, and resource commitment to be successful. It must be suited to the organization's situation so that it can become a fundamental part of the organization, or it will become just another fad, forgotten as soon as something new comes along or top management changes.

Applying total quality methods to accounting occupies the next few chapters of this book. There are no magic cure-alls, but there are some possibilities for improving the ways work is approached, the way specific tasks are done, and the products delivered to accounting's customers.

SETTING UP A TQM ORGANIZATIONAL PATTERN

All of us who are parts of organizations have seen the lines of authority depicted on organization charts. We looked to the established authorities for instruction, guidance, permission, and validation of our actions. TQM doesn't eliminate these authority structures, but gives them new legitimacy by using the ingenuity and accumulated experience of the workers. Although it is rightly said that no one knows the work like the worker, accountants and clerks in a TQM implementation will still report to their supervisors, managers, and the company's chief accounting officer. They will, however, have increased ability to contribute by working smarter as they apply their knowledge and experience to work design, product design, and coordination of effort.

One result of applying everyone's abilities can be the reorganization of the accounting department into product lines (like payables, payroll, and financial accounting), processes (like data entry, report generation, and special analyses), or customer service groups (like marketing accounting, production accounting, and purchasing accounting).

The prevalent organization pattern today is by *product line*, with an accounting section for each product. For example, one product is disbursement checks, or, increasingly, electronic payments. To produce them, there is a separate accounts payable function; if the organization is large enough, the section will have its own office spaces and supervisor. The same pattern is used for payroll checks and a payroll department, billing and an accounts receivable section, financial reports and a financial accounting section, or cost reports and a cost accounting section. This form of organization is traditional, and has proven useful in many cases. It parallels the manufacturing approach of linear flow using manufacturing cells as each transaction moves from input to output in a single work group.

Another form of organization is *process organization*, where workers are physically located and supervised according to what they do. Data processing departments are usually set up like this, with operations, programming, hardware maintenance, and user support in separate sections. An accounting department using this pattern might have data entry, analysis, and report preparation in separate sections. Here, all mail, time cards, and other source documents would go to a single department for entry into the company's records, presumably through electronic terminals. Another section would prepare and analyze data by assigning account codes for classification and summary. Still another would review the classified and summarized data to determine what was worth reporting, while report design and preparation might be another function. This form is seen in practice only in the case of certain specialized skills, such as some data entry or cost analysis sections.

The last organizational form is by *customer* and is often used where each accountant is assigned specific customers. These accountants are usually located with the accounting customer, as in the cases of division controllers or plant accountants who handle accounting, review, and analysis for the workers and managers in each plant. Even in such cases, however, bookkeeping services, bill paying, and billing of customers is usually provided by a central department at the home office, and it is usually organized in the product-oriented pattern described first. Dual lines of authority are often used where there are site accountants, with technical direction coming from the corporate controller and daily direction and supervision coming from the plant or division manager.

There is no universal best TQM pattern of formal organization. In fact, it isn't likely to be a good idea to reorganize during TQM implementation unless the TQM process itself yields reorganization as a solution to specific situations. This is because reorganizing will eliminate the basis of comparing new techniques with old ones. As noted earlier, we will have no consistent process from which to get before and after data, so we can't answer Dr. Deming's question "How do you know?"

Another reason for not upsetting the existing expectations and authority structures is that each new report format or data processing technique will have to be implemented after it's designed. Resources will have to be assigned to the implementation. Tasks will have to be reapportioned. These will have to be assigned by someone with authority to command the resources. The work group will look to established authorities for such resource direction. Even after work groups have established permanent quality circles and begun using problem-solving teams, the improvements suggested by the teams must be put into action. When the formally designated supervisor directs that a group's recommendation become the new way of working, it legitimizes the supervisor's authority at the same time it empowers the workers. Such recognition is the most effective "pat on the back" anyone can receive. It reinforces the supervisor while reinforcing the workers. In cases where a supervisor feels that a recommendation needs more work, even the act of asking for further refinement of a recommendation shows both that the supervisor is the leader and that the workers are valued for their experience and ideas.

Further, we should probably keep existing formal structures because TQM is enough of a change in company culture; most of us like change, but not too much all at once. Retaining familiar structure is comforting and gives confidence. Finally, because TQM empowers workers, there can be an early tendency to anarchy; retaining the existing structure gives the process a source of discipline and order that is necessary for a data-driven management style.

Using established structures means that the controller will still report to the financial vice-president or president and will still be responsible for accurate, timely reporting of useful data to operating and staff sections. Accounting departments will still be responsible for support services like payroll, supplier payments, billing, and receipts processing. These tasks must be carried out efficiently and accurately. TQM is a means to becoming a better, more effective, and more efficient accounting function. It is not a substitute for structure, order, and discipline. If anything, it demands more.

Thus, typical lines of authority running from the controller to accounting, reporting, and service functions will not be disturbed by TQM implementation, but will be enhanced by it under the usual TQM pattern. Even if the TQM process yields reorganization as a means of improving accounting products and processes, the new structures will also be orderly with clear responsibility assignments for each group or individual.

QUALITY CIRCLES IN THE ACCOUNTING FUNCTION

Readers who have encountered quality circles before may have heard them called quality management boards, quality councils, methods study groups, or other names. The name, *quality circle*, is the oldest, being a direct translation of the Japanese name for worker groups that meet regularly to determine how to improve work processes. Because it was the first name used, "quality circle" unfortunately has been associated with faddish attempts to establish quality circles without really changing the company culture. Such circles, without supporting procedures or management commitment, too often died out without producing the quick improvements their instigators hoped for. Consequently, another name might be best in your company, though the old name "quality circle" will be used here for continuity.

In self-directed work teams, the work of the quality circle is one of the main functions of the team. In more conventional organizational patterns, circles exist within work groups, but the total quality structure, with its quality circles, is parallel to the conventional pattern rather than replacing it.

Whatever name a particular organization may choose, it should be selected by the members of the organization itself, so that the name will be part of the new company quality culture. While it need not be unique to the company, it should not be adopted copy-cat fashion, but should be chosen or created to reflect both the company's accepted outlook and its new direction. This will encourage ownership of the total quality implementation process and aid in viewing things in a new light.

Recall that the work of quality circles is to find improvement opportunities in their work processes. They do not exist to gripe about working conditions. Sometimes it is hard to keep a discussion of productivity and quality barriers from deteriorating into such gripe sessions, because obstacles to quality work are also sources of dissatisfaction on the job. Thorough training and skilled leadership by the chairman (the work section supervisor) are needed to impose necessary discipline without quashing useful discussion.

In addition, recent legal decisions have found that if such groups focus on working conditions, they are "company unions" and are illegal under labor laws. An exception to the law may be sought, but has not yet been enacted.

Meetings are typically held weekly. Holding them more often detracts from the primary work of the section; holding them less often leads to forgetting, so each meeting must take time to reacquaint members with the subjects under continuing discussion. The ability to receive progress reports from appointed action teams each week also imposes discipline on the action teams to get their work done and to adhere to their assignments' objectives and restrictions.

Discipline is also imposed by using a prepared agenda for the discussion at each meeting. The quality circle leader should keep an agenda through the week between meetings. Since the leader is also the formal supervisor, he or she is a natural focal point to whom to bring agenda items as improvement opportunities arise.

At quality circle meetings themselves, the leader steers the circle through the agenda. Such leadership requires skills that most of us didn't get in school or in conventional work experiences. Consequently, training is necessary, and this is another function of external consultants or, in large enough companies, an internal total quality implementation function.

The leaders, being supervisors of work sections, together make up the next level quality circle, along with the controller. They also meet weekly and consider topics that could not be resolved by the section quality circles as well as new topics that members of the supervisory circle feel will offer improvement opportunities for the whole department.

Topics brought up at a quality circle meeting at any level may be resolved on the spot, under the authority of the leader who is also the section supervisor. If approval from higher levels is needed, the supervisor can get it either through normal channels or by bringing the matter to the next meeting of the accounting supervisors' circle.

Another possible disposition of a quality circle topic is that it might come up initially at a supervisors' circle meeting, and be referred to others closer to the situation, such as the payroll section or analysis section circles. Alternatively, a matter might require more study than can be given in one- or two-hour meetings each week. Particularly if not everyone needs to be involved in the study, an action team can be appointed.

When an improvement is agreed upon by the members, it must be put into effect. For this, it is necessary that someone with the authority to make changes in procedures, policies, manuals, and resource allocations direct the required changes. The formal supervisor, as the quality circle leader, has such authority in many cases. In other cases the supervisor can obtain the required changes through normal approval processes.

Thus, while total quality management is a new way of achieving continuous improvement, it does not necessarily do away with the structure of the organization. It does not destroy what already is effective, but instead uses it for even better management. It is especially important not to overthrow existing lines of authority in accounting work, because accounting is essential to disciplined management throughout the company. Upsetting the certainty of accounting methods and products upsets the whole management of the organization. If improvements are made, but not understood by "customers," they will be worse than no improvements, since they will be misinterpreted and may mislead management in directing the company's business.

To help follow all this, here's a concrete example:

Billing Section Quality Circle

Supervisor (1)
Billing associates (3)
Collections section representative (1)
Sales department representative (1)
Treasury (cash management) representative (1)

Meeting Schedule

Each Thursday 1:00 to 2:30

Sample Agenda

1. "Out of memory" indications running reports.
2. When talking to customers and advancing through customer accounts on screen, cannot back up to previous screens.

---

3. Customers complain of difficulty processing invoices because charges list in service order number only.

(These agenda items were accumulated during the week between meetings by the quality circle leader, using forms submitted by circle members.)

Synopsis of Discussion

After introducing a new member representing the treasury cash management function, the leader opened discussing by asking the associate who submitted item #1, "out of memory" indications to describe the problem that interferes with productivity.

Members suggested adding memory to the workstation, removing old data from files so they would fit in available memory, and replacing the workstation. Another suggestion was to examine the programs for inefficient use of memory.

The circle decided to appoint the associate who pointed out the problem to a team with a data processing representative and a programmer to determine the best approach and to report on progress weekly, with a final recommendation within four weeks. The leader was to contact the data processing department for team members in service and programming.

The problem of inability to retrace all data in a customer account while talking to customers was resolved by submitting a Program Change Request form to the data processing department. The leader signed the request on the spot and forwarded it to data processing with a copy to the suggestor for reference. Under this company's procedures, the data processing department must respond with intended actions within five working days, so a report of intentions should be available at the next meeting or the one after that.

The last barrier to productivity to be discussed was that customers complained of difficulty breaking down charges for their internal accounting needs. The circle decided to appoint a team to determine exactly which customers needed invoice changes, what changes would be useful to them, and how such changes could be made. Two billing section associates and the collections representative were appointed to the team, with authority to request data processing assistance if needed at the "how to make changes" stage.

Subsequent Actions

The "out of memory" problem team determined that files could not be reduced because all the historical data was needed. A new workstation could be provided that would work faster as well as provide added memory. Upgrading memory in the existing workstation was also possible, but would provide no speed advantage. Program changes would take up to three months. The team's choice was to install added memory, with the section supervisor's approval, in the workstation for the associate who normally ran the reports in question. The installation was done by the service representative on the problem study team in about an hour at a material cost of $30 for memory chips.

The inability to retrace through screens after they had once been viewed while researching a customer's account was determined to require computer program changes. Since a new release of the programs was due in a few months, and it was planned to include "back" capability, no programming was requested. Instead, it was decided as an interim measure to get callers' phone numbers. The billing associate would then print an account history on the local printer before calling back. The printed history would allow associates to scan the whole account. The call-back procedure would also allow contact with the collections section and sales, if indicated, to ensure a consistent story in dealing with customers.

The last productivity issue, of invoice content and design, was dealt with by referring it to the department level quality circle, where supervisors of all accounting functions would be present along with data processing, treasury, and sales representatives. The higher-level quality circle in turn referred it higher yet to ensure participation by all affected parties in dealing with a problem experienced by some of the company's ultimate customers, and to ensure that the customer received a positive experience in the contact.

Looking over this example, it can be seen that these are the kinds of problems that most companies would either address slowly, through procedures that might break down at any point in the chain, or would not address at all, leaving associates to cope as best they could. With the quality circle, each was considered in an atmosphere that provided open discussion, a number of associates and skill areas to contribute to solutions, documentation of action taken, and follow-up. Accountability for progress was also established.

In this way none of the responsibilities of management were abrogated, but workers' skills and abilities were enlisted in solving their own problems. The supervisor's leadership was reinforced as she became more than just an order-giver. Instead, she was able to become an enabler of others and add power and adaptability to the organization. Assistance was available when needed, and progress reporting was provided. These advantages are why quality circles are part of every total quality management implementation.

ACCOUNTING ACTION TEAMS

Because accounting cuts through all areas of a company, it is often apparent at quality circles that members don't have enough data from other areas to know what solutions are possible, or even whether an apparent opportunity is real. In addition, it sometimes happens that an obvious solution for one work group is a source of problems for others. A manager and his immediate subordinates may be too far removed from handling actual data to know all the ramifications and possible solutions.

In such cases, where cross-functional solutions are needed or where there isn't enough data, improvement opportunities are handled through action teams. Each team is formed for the purpose of answering a specific question. ("What should be done about the erroneous material issues on the gearbox line?") Unlike quality circles, which are permanent, teams are formed for a specific question and that question only. If they discover other questions not within their original purpose, they must refer them to the chartering circle for appointment of a new team or obtain a new charter to consider these questions as part of their assignment.

An action team working on some facet of cost accounting relevance, perhaps on bases for allocating production overhead, will include representatives of the departments whose work is described in the reports, such as production shops and staffs. It will include expert representatives such as production engineers and it will include representatives of the report's customers, such as a production manager, along with the cost accountants.

Topics suitable for accounting department action teams include improvement opportunities that remove barriers to productivity and effectiveness in accounting processes, such as automation opportunities, selecting accounting software, electronic data interchange, and internal processing methods. They can also include improvement opportunities that primarily concern accounting functions, but that affect the whole company's ways of interpreting and acting on data, such as activity-based costing projects, distinguishing relevant costs, and report design.

To see how an action team can work, let's continue the example of customers who have difficulty paying from the invoices we send:

Invoice Improvement Action Team

Chartering Quality Circle

Billing section
Accounting department

Charter

Determine why certain customers cannot process our invoices in their accounts payable systems, delaying payments and harming customer relations. Devise an improved invoice format and outline steps in its implementation, including cost and time estimates.

Members

(Names are listed in the actual charter, positions are listed here.)

Billing section associates (2)
Data processing department programmer (1)
Sales associate (1)
Collections section associate (1)

Timetable

Interim reports, biweekly
Findings of fact, September 21
Recommendations, October 12

With this charter and with members assigned, the action team began to develop its approach to the problem. Copies of the charter were also sent to the TQM implementation office and to the accounting department quality circle. Department heads who were asked to supply team members also received copies with their requests for personnel assignment. The team made up the following plan of action and a timetable, which was forwarded to the sponsoring quality circle as the first biweekly report:

Invoice Improvement Team Plan of Action

1. Survey customers as to source of difficulty and preferred invoice format.
2. Develop an invoice format that meets customer needs.
3. Request customer validation of proposed new format.
4. Revise internal procedures to provide data needed for revised format (if changes in other processes are needed, request approval for changes from affected functions).
5. Schedule systems reprogramming as needed.
6. Validate operation of new procedures and program changes.
7. Revalidate with customers.
8. Adopt new format as company standard.

When the billing section quality circle accepted the plan of action, the team assigned members to carry out the steps. It also established a regular meeting schedule to review progress, and dates were set.

As part of the survey of customers, the billing representatives on the team identified specific customers who had complained of problems dealing with invoices. The collections representative and the sales representative then selected those customers along with a sampling of others to develop a new format that would serve customers better.

It turned out that most customers were satisfied, but those who needed more information didn't really have problems with the invoices so much as with their own internal procedures. They were all customers who used our services on a number of jobs, and they needed to account for our services by job. Since we rendered a consolidated invoice, these customers had to circulate it to all the project managers to obtain approval of the charges.

Customers who used purchase orders didn't have this difficulty with our invoices since we issued a separate invoice for each customer purchase order number, and the customers could send them to the project manager who had ordered the services. Only customers who called us for services without any single point of contact or tracking system (such as purchase orders) had this problem.

The team was able to resolve the issues quickly from that point by instructing the order desk to always obtain either a purchase order number or the name of the individual who ordered a service. Then, the name was entered in the purchase order space on our records and on the invoices, and our existing procedures produced a separate invoice for each distinct purchase order number entry.

In this way, customers had to route each invoice to only one person in their organization to have the charges identified. Where the ordering person was one of their project managers who had only one project, the charge was obvious even without routing the invoice. Eliminating the need for these customers to hand our invoices around their organizations for multiple approvals not only speeded the routing in terms of number of hands through which they had to pass, but no single problem or delay could hold up payment on all the charges that had formerly been consolidated on a single invoice.

To ensure that this change was adhered to, a program change was initiated to require an entry in the purchase order field whenever an order was entered. Even if the order-taker entered something like "000," some conscious attention to the matter was required. It couldn't be ignored altogether.

When the action team made its recommendation to the billing section quality circle, the recommendation was accepted and forwarded through the circle's leader, the supervisor, to the controller and then to the sales and data processing departments for approval of procedural and program changes.

After full approval and implementation, it was published in the internal quality newsletter as a "good example" for those involved. It was eventually exported to other sites of the company.

This change was much simpler and easier than first appeared when the team was appointed. Asking customers what would help them generated goodwill, as we demonstrated our customer-oriented approach to business. It required only a minimal program and procedural change in taking orders, and it reduced billing and collection section workloads while speeding customer payments.

Without quality circles it is unlikely that this problem would ever have received proper consideration. Without an action team, it is unlikely that the affected parties would ever have gotten together to work out a permanent, comprehensive solution to this problem. Using these total quality tools in the accounting function brings about many small improvements like this one, so that accounting becomes ever more responsive to the organization and its customers. Accounting functions are carried out more efficiently and with fewer errors as workers have fewer problems in their work processes. The continuous improvement environment that is total quality management yields few giant leaps, but many small steps toward reliable processes and responsive products. Action teams are an effective way to bring about improvements in an accounting function and are an integral, necessary part of every total quality implementation.

TQM TRAINING FOR ACCOUNTANTS

We've seen that a complete revolution in managerial outlook is needed in order for total quality management to produce its full range of benefits. We have to believe (or at least act as though we believe) that a fraction of each week spent talking with others about how to work better and smarter is more valuable than another hour of working harder. We have to know what to do in quality circle meetings to get maximum productive effect. We have to know what resources are available to help us. As described in part 1, skilled facilitators are helpful in each group's first few meetings.

In an accounting function, the basic training package given to all workers is the necessary starting point. To succeed, we must share a common understanding and feeling of teamwork and of adventure that comes with common training. But more is needed as well. While accounting products can and must be evaluated objectively, they also have a large component of subjective worth in the eyes of each user. We must be trained to discover value in the eyes of our customers, then to find ways to provide it. The tools for doing so were discussed in the first part of this text. These tools can be provided and adapted by the TQM implementation team in each company.

We also need training in how to conduct a quality circle meeting, what an action team's responsibilities are, and many other things. Without training and without a skilled facilitator (at least at early quality circle and action team meetings) we risk so much undirected activity that TQM begins to look like a "touchy-feely" program. Productivity of the TQM process, like any productivity, requires direction, discipline, and skill. In other words, we need adequate training.

Credibility is essential for any management change to be effective. Credibility in commercial organizations comes from two sources: evidence of past success and upper management support. Evidence of success will be provided during the training of each work group by examining what other companies and other countries have accomplished. In many cases, tours can be arranged of plants or facilities that have had success with TQM, including briefings by workers in positions similar to those of the visitors.

If a company engages a consultant, he or she can be another source of success stories. The consultant can often provide examples from personal experience as well as from literature and acquaintances. Where the total quality implementation has taken place in phases, internal successes are probably available and are especially credible.

The other primary source of credibility is upper management support. Since no amount of preaching is worth as much as leadership by example, the upper management group must be first to attend training in total quality concepts and practices. The first quality circles must be held among the top management group members. Then they can begin circles in their separate departments with full confidence and credibility.

Since the chief financial officer and the controller will be among the first to receive total quality training, the accounting department should be brought into the total quality program early in the implementation. Unfortunately, that is not done as often as it should be because most companies are anxious to deploy their resources directly in the products and services that they deliver to their customers. The TQM emphasis on customer satisfaction makes such an approach fitting, of course, but it sometimes leaves the accounting department "out of the loop." Here is where it can be helpful to engage another consultant for administrative functions, so that someone devotes substantial time to these areas and so that someone with experience in total quality accounting is available in addition to the usual production experts.

Another reason it is important to train accountants along with production personnel is that the production group will want to focus their first efforts where customer service can be improved at least cost. Later, they will also want to know the cost effects of their improvement efforts. To know the costs requires accounting products that meet the total quality management requirements of being customer focused, participatively developed (including the production departments that will use them), and data driven. Accounting products can be truly accepted by total quality production workers only if they are also produced in a total quality environment.

Once we recognize that total quality training for accountants is needed early in a TQM implementation, the immediate questions are: "How should the training be phased through the hierarchy?" and "What should be the content of the training?"

The answer to the first question was touched upon when we noted that it begins with the top management group. As soon as the controller has received practical training, the accounting supervisors can be given awareness training. When the controller has begun to function as a member of the executive quality circle with other upper management members, practical training can be given to the accounting supervisors and a quality circle can be organized with the controller and accounting supervisors.

To get ready to give total quality service, accountants need the same training as other organization members and in the same phases. Those phases should be:

1. Awareness training;
2. A survey of techniques (often given as quality circles are forming); and
3. Applications and skills (often given as actual quality issues are dealt with in quality circles and action teams).

Let's look briefly at each of these phases.

Awareness Training

The first training area in TQM is awareness training. In this stage, the managers and workers are introduced to total quality concepts and their possible successes. A seminar like the Deming seminar or another taught by recognized experts can be a good introduction. Alternatively, more readily accessible local trainers can be used, supplemented by videotapes and written material if desired. This is the stage where popular books can be introduced, such as *Quality Is Free*, or *If Japan Can, Why Can't We?*, or *Deming Management at Work*. Books from the Peters "Excellence" series can also be helpful, particularly in their emphasis on customer service. These are just a few of the books available on TQM.

Memberships in the American Society for Quality Control, the American Production and Inventory Control Society, and the American Productivity Center are excellent for any member of a total quality organization, and there are often "user groups" in local areas as well. For accountants specifically, the Institute of Management Accountants is a good choice, particularly its Continuous Improvement Center. The AICPA has a benchmarking project underway. Any of these organizations can offer course materials, courses, and books to assist in the awareness phase of training.

It is important too that everyone participate, especially at the top levels. It will do no good to tell subordinates "You need this total quality stuff!" if the boss doesn't care enough to be trained and to begin practicing total quality management. When subordinates see higher-level workers learning and developing total quality awareness and skills, they are eager to join in too. If it's all talk and no action by the upper management group and every other level leading to a particular worker, it looks like just another fad being begun by pronouncement, but not backed up with real commitment.

Techniques

As the levels of the organization become aware of total quality principles and practices, they will want to form their first quality circles as a way of putting the new ideas into practice. This leads into the second phase of training, survey of total quality management techniques. These techniques may have been introduced briefly in the awareness phase of training, but in this phase the emphasis will be shifted to their practical use. Since this phase is likely to coincide with the formation of quality circles, it will provide the new quality circles with a "laundry list" of methods that can be used to attack the barriers to quality and productivity that are raised on the circles' agenda.

Application Skills

As soon as a quality circle or action team believes it needs to use one of the TQM techniques to deal with an actual issue, it will require assistance in assuring that the technique it has chosen is really right for the situation and in applying the selected technique to the concrete facts.

At this point, the quality consulting group, either outside consultants or an internal group, should be available to provide the necessary training and to lead the circles or teams through their first real use of TQM on a specific problem. Learning by doing is the best way to absorb specific techniques, and learning total quality applications and skills through resolving real problems is without parallel as an opportunity for such training. This is the same principle that has been described for teaching the operation of quality circles and action teams, where expert assistance is available to facilitate the early meetings of each new circle and team.

In some cases, management will want to introduce a total quality technique to a whole work section at once, especially the use of statistical process control charts and like methods that can be applied continuously as work progresses. In these cases, it is still best for each worker to learn by doing, preferably by constructing charts with his or her own data for actual use in daily work.

Technical Accounting Training

A final remark on training in total quality management for accountants is that the methods of total quality management can make better accounting products and processes, but only if the accountants know how to do accounting in the first place. Continuing accounting education is a requirement for constant improvement in accounting functions. Membership in professional organizations has already been mentioned. Certification such as Certified Public Accountant (CPA), Certified Management Accountant (CMA), or Chartered Internal Auditor (CIA) are evidence of accounting theoretical knowledge as well as of practical ability. The continuing education requirements of these designations help assure that the techniques of total quality management have the necessary basic material to build upon in making better products from the accounting department and better processes within it.

ACCOUNTING TRAINING FOR NON-FINANCIAL MANAGERS AND ASSOCIATES

We have just seen that accountants need total quality management training in order to assist their non-financial associates in using accounting information. We now turn the question around, and see how to help those associates understand what is available from an accounting department.

In a total quality facility, each associate accepts responsibility for his own work. It is management's job to provide tools and opportunities for each worker to discharge this responsibility. One requirement for effectively discharging these responsibilities is an ability to interpret the classified and summarized operating data that the accounting system reports. Unfortunately, operating personnel too often cannot properly interpret accounting information, and sometimes have given up trying, claiming that the reports are not relevant. Publications that serve operations managers often carry complaints that accounting reports don't reflect the activities of their departments and shops. Even where operations managers are aware of the relationships between their actions and the cost allocations they see on their accounting reports, they feel that cost allocations are arbitrary and not related to the decisions or actions of line management. Whether these impressions are valid or not, they interfere with effective use of the information that is available. Such impressions are also barriers to cooperation among operating and staff departments.

Part 2 of this text offered accounting methods that could improve the relationship between accounting reports and actions taken by line managers. Regrettably, line managers either don't know that such techniques are available, or if they recognize the names, they lack sufficient acquaintance with these methods to request useful changes.

A way out of the dilemma is to use the total quality structure to bring operating managers and workers in as members of accounting department quality circles and action teams. At the same time, accountants should offer to join

circles and teams in operating departments. Even with this channel of cooperation open, operating managers will need some understanding of the economic effects of their actions. Achieving the necessary understanding is possible through a program that includes practical economics and accounting as
part of the job skills training that is given to each member of the organization. If associates and managers resist spending time with economics, which
often seems too hard, or with accounting, which sometimes seems too
"bookish," try calling it "engineering economy." An engineer could even
teach the class, so long as it includes enough accounting to meet line managers' needs when they have to deal with their accounting information.

So just as in the previous discussion of what accountants need to know about
TQM, we have two questions to answer about accounting education for non-
financial members of our organizations: "How should the training be phased
through the hierarchy?" and "What should be the content of the training?"

When to Train Users in Accounting and Economics

The answer to the first question, "How should the training be phased through
the hierarchy?," is that it should be included as part of the basic job skills
training given to each member of an organization. In total quality companies,
skills are continuously developed and upgraded through regular training, typically given just before the practical skill will be used.

For managers, economics and accounting can be included in a basic skills
package that would include hiring and personnel management, planning,
time management, and other similar management skills. While it may seem
that any supervisor or manager would already have such skills, it is surpris-
ing how many of us have voids in our knowledge of some basic functional
areas of business.

In any event, a total quality organization provides training for all its associates as a way of continually improving its products and processes, including the abilities of managers and workers.

To give such training just before it will be used means, in most cases, giving it after TQM awareness training and after the survey of TQM techniques.
Usually the best time is just as quality circles are forming, or right after they
form. Then, when cost-related topics come up in circle discussions, false reasoning will be minimized and the circle members will be aware of the information available to help them.

Training in economics and accounting is essential before adopting *open
accounting*, covered in detail later, where virtually all financial and cost
information can be reviewed by anyone in the company. A reduced-scope
variation is one wherein information about an associate's own work unit (and

any subordinate units for managers) is available, but not information on other units.

Further, just as workers must see that executives and managers take seriously their training in total quality principles, economics and accounting education must start at the top. A program where each executive sets up a course for her peers, explaining her areas of responsibility, is one way to achieve such training for an executive-level group.

To summarize the question of when to give accounting training to non-financial personnel, such training should be an integral part of the skill base for every job in a total quality organization. Only by knowing the cost implications can wise choices be made by quality circles and action teams. While cost cannot be the only factor considered, and will often be a minor one, it must be based on accurate interpretation of available information. Where available information is inadequate to a circle or team's task, awareness of that fact and of what other information could be produced is essential to optimum effectiveness. Consequently, training in accounting for non-financial associates should be given at each level of the company as quality circles begin their work at that level.

What Accounting Training for Users Should Include

The second question, "What should be the content of the training?" is easier to answer, at least for an accountant, but more complex in execution.

W. Edwards Deming, a founder of the total quality movement, said that practices must be based on sound theory. Only when the basic principles are well understood can we develop practices that will work together and withstand the test of changing circumstances. Consequently, we should begin with theory, and at a basic level. After defining terms, cost-volume-profit analysis will be seen to contain all the concepts needed for most members of an organization. It includes fixed costs, variable costs, and causal relationships. It integrates these factors as necessary parts of the simple calculation that wraps up the subject.

Each worker should learn to do cost-volume-profit calculations, if possible, using data from his own work section. It isn't necessary to become proficient, but going through the exercise ensures that the concept is understood and reinforced through a practical application. Later, when actual opportunities for improvement surface in daily work, they will be viewed through a proper knowledge of economic principles, and correct conclusions are far more likely.

Since the accounting information that is circulated in most companies today includes allocation of fixed costs, it is also necessary to acquaint total quality management workers with the kinds of cost allocations that are made and what the alternatives are. Then, the common error of treating fixed costs as if they were variable can be avoided. Too often, even sophisticated managers remove steps from production, then wonder why they haven't seen the promised savings. As shown in part 2, reallocating fixed costs to the remaining production does not make them go away. Proper training in these subjects can avoid such reasoning mistakes.

Another area where accounting information is commonly used by line departments' quality circles is in developing recommendations for investment in new capital equipment. Although experience shows that quality circles are more likely to find low-cost, quickly applied "fixes," they also sometimes find new equipment, facilities, or floor layouts are helpful in improving their processes. In these cases, capital investment analysis is needed, with its accompanying complications of discounted cash flow, internal rates of return, and cost of capital. It is not necessary to train all associates in such calculations, but they should be aware of them so that they can ask for assistance when necessary. The value of accounting representation on line department quality circles and action teams will quickly become evident to operating managers when such cases arise. This opportunity to become an integral part of operating management should not be missed, and a key to achieving it is education for non-financial personnel so that they realize the need for such services as a component of improving their own products and processes.

Trained Managers Will Ask for Better Information

When operating managers and workers begin to meet in quality circles, they are likely to use their new knowledge to swamp the accounting department with requests for more relevant information. This should be expected and anticipated by preparing a structure for making analyses of the kinds likely to be most asked for. Alterations in the chart of accounts or job cost systems might be needed to collect data in categories that will be useful in economic analysis.

Traditional absorption costing using labor-based allocations is fine for financial reports to outsiders, but it won't do for total quality managers and workers. They will demand information that more accurately reflects their actions, or they will soon ignore the accounting department and develop their own information. The duplicate reporting structures needed to do this are unnecessary and expensive. They add to the operator's workload and complicate his job. Reporting relevant and useful economic information is the purpose of management accounting, and accountants in total quality organizations will be compelled to serve their customers. Total quality accountants will anticipate the needs of their internal customers and will be ready with the kinds of information that will assist the company on its march into the new, more demanding marketplace. The phasing of training to follow the implementation of quality circles ensures that staff sections like accounting, with typically fewer layers, will get training throughout the department ahead of the operating departments, and have an opportunity to prepare.

Conclusion

It is evident, then, that training for accountants in total quality methods, training for non-financial associates in basic economics, and the phased implementation of total quality management all go together as a single, integrated program. That is really what TQM is all about—getting the whole organization to pull together in the single direction of customer satisfaction. The accounting function and the kinds of information that it provides are an essential part of that pulling together. It must be included as an integral part of the training that takes place throughout a total quality implementation.

8

WHAT THE CUSTOMER WANTS AT A PRICE HE IS WILLING TO PAY

As we've seen, the goal of training is an effective TQM process, and the goal of TQM is higher quality services for our customers. There are many such customers to consider. Some accounting customers are within the company and some are outside it. Anyone who uses a piece of paper or an electronic file created or altered by accounting is a customer. Bankers, stockholders, regulatory authorities, the shop supervisor, the supplier who gets a check, and the customer who gets a bill are all accounting customers.

To give the customer what he wants, we must first find out what that is. We can read customer specifications if they are furnished, we can observe what kinds of questions are asked about information already sent, and we can ask users directly what they want. In short, we can do market research.

Some tools that were mentioned in Part 1 can be adapted for this purpose. These tools include the Delphi technique, the nominal group technique, focus groups, and surveys. The TQM implementation group can also help identify customer needs and expectations.

Another source of information on customer needs in a total quality management implementation is the customer representatives on our quality circles and action teams. These quality circle members are there specifically to tell us what the customer wants; they should be fully utilized for this purpose as well as for their specialized and general skills. Soliciting helpful, willing customer representatives for our circles and teams is one of the key challenges of TQM.

When customers' wishes become known, the issue of cost of information also deserves attention. Indirect costs have traditionally been allocated according to labor hours or dollars. In these cases, the added cost of one work section's new information is allocated to all work sections. This hides the information cost so well that it looks like free goods to the person requesting it. The misapprehension that information is free will be corrected if the total quality revolution leads a company to adopt cost assignment schemes that more accurately follow causal links. Then, these costs should find their way to the work section that asked for information.

Another advantage of including customers in quality circles and action teams is that they can place values on the accounting products they receive. Customers can tell us which changes are important and worth the cost of changing and which changes are not worthwhile. Under alternative cost assignment schemes such as direct costing or activity-based costing, added costs become explicit. With activity-based costing, they will be assigned to the work section that benefits from the information. Not all companies will adopt these improved management accounting techniques right away, but when they do, the cost-benefit comparison will be forced on operating units that request accounting efforts. In this way, continuous process value analysis is applied. Accounting products no longer look like free goods, and the incentive to use them effectively is increased. Customers may also offer suggestions on whether to continue producing current products. The normal flow of discussion provides many of the benefits of process value analysis without the added cost, as quality circle and action team members from customer and accounting sections compare costs and benefits while looking for new ways of meeting the company's needs.

Recognizing that our customers are the focus of our efforts, it's time to look at a few of them in detail. In the following sections, customers will be examined in order from top management to the shop floor. A few accounting customers from outside the organization will also be discussed.

OUR MOST INFLUENTIAL CUSTOMERS:
THE CEO AND UPPER MANAGEMENT TEAM

Of all the users of accounting products, the most influential is the chief executive officer. If the CEO is an engineer, he is probably absorbed by the engineering and production aspects of the business. If he is a sales representative or marketer, he is likely to be absorbed by those areas. Either way, CEOs often show little interest in accounting. Consequently, accounting products are sometimes discounted as too late, too general, and too full of arbitrary allocations. The CEO sets this tone, so becoming a more valued part of the organization means convincing the CEO that accounting can contribute significantly to its success.

In most TQM implementations, the CEO will be chairman of the executive quality circle with the chief financial officer (CFO) as a member.

Executive quality circle meetings offer an opportunity to gain support and credibility for the accounting function through energetic participation. Participating fully as a team player in the executive quality circle can open the door to equal priority with other staff functions and to the cooperation of others when accounting issues are on the agenda.

While the CEO is the most influential individual customer, the most influential customer group is the whole upper management team, and it is the one most likely to benefit from improving the relevance of accounting products. Pleasing our upper management customers means producing one-time studies and analyses that are timely, clear, and relevant. It also means that scheduled reporting must be prompt and readable. Because of their broad-based orientation, viewing the business as a whole, upper management is a customer group that uses financial accounting reports as well as cost accounting analyses and special studies such as capital investment analyses.

To find which of these products are most valued and which of their features are most in need of improvement, the simplest way is to ask. Their time is at a premium, so a general questionnaire may be viewed by upper management as a low priority. Instead, questions must be specific, possibly referring to exact layouts and lines of specific reports. A good way to get such questions before the user is to send them with the report itself, possibly including them right on the face of a second copy (see Figures 8-1 and 8-2).

The sample questionnaire shown might be used early in a total quality implementation, to accompany the statement shown here with it, before more sophisticated cost accounting changes as direct costing or activity-based costing have been accepted.

These questionnaires will usually be sponsored by the accounting department quality circle and produced by an action team chartered for the purpose. Another approach is to save the reader the effort of creative thought in an area (in this instance accounting reports) that is not part of his primary expertise. This can be done by presenting alternative formats and asking the reader to choose among them. More work is required of the accounting department circles or teams, but less is required of the upper management users. The "Request for Quality Review" shown in Figure 8-3 can be modified to fit the company's specific working style and the specific content of the report under review.

When we have gathered all the "market research" data available, the accounting department quality circle, its subordinate quality circles, or action teams can study each product for ways to improve the product itself and the process of creating it. The results of this work may then be presented to the executive quality circle or to a specially convened validation panel for final validation.

In summary, we can get upper management involved with our accounting products and processes and we can please these customers with our products

Figure 8-1. Management Questionnaire to Improve the Quality of Plant Operating Statements.

To improve the usefulness of our products for you, our customer, we want to know how this operating statement can be made more productive for you. Of course, we want any comments you may offer, but to simplify your response, we have also provided some prepared questions.

Please take a few moments as you read this operating statement to respond to the questions and jot down any comments you may have.

Thank you in advance for your assistance as we strive to improve everything we do here at the Goofus Corporation.

Sam Hill
Controller

Line 1—
   Would you also like the range of prices at which sales were made?   Y   N

Line 5—
   Would you like direct labor hours as well as dollars, both total and per unit?   Y   N

Line 6—
   Would you like direct costs per unit, before production indirect costs are added? Y   N

Lines 11 and 12—
   Would you like a brief enumeration on this report of selling and general & administrative costs by major cost type (salaries & wages, commissions, occupancy charges, communication costs, equipment costs)?   Y   N

Please also give a rating to this report as to the following characteristics. Please rate them on a 0-10 scale (0 = terrible, 10 = perfect).

| Relevance | _____ | Completeness | _____ |
| Readability | _____ | Clarity | _____ |

Please add any additional comments to the back of this questionnaire and return it by folding it in thirds and stapling it so the address on the back side is readable. Thank you again for your help!

by active participation in the TQM process, by observing what is used, by asking what is wanted, and by bringing issues to the executive quality circle wherever the nature of a problem demands it. We can also invite members of the executive quality circle to sit in on sessions of the accounting quality circle occasionally, particularly when a topic may be one to which they can contribute.

In these ways, we can interest the chief executive and the upper management group in opportunities for improvements in the accounting function,

Figure 8-2. Operating Statement: Frammis Plant. July

		Dollars		Units	Per Unit
1	**Sales**		$2,138,000	1,638	$1,305
	Cost of Sales:				
2	Beginning Inventory		$ 135,000	201	$672
3	Goods Manufactured				
4	Direct Material	$585,000			
5	Direct Labor	$302,000			
6	Production Indirect	$212,000			
7	Total Goods Manufactured	$1,099,000		1,675	$656
8	Goods Available for Sale	$1,234,000		1,876	$658
9	Less: Ending Inventory	($147,319)	$1,086,681	(224)	$658
10	**Gross Profit:**		$1,051,319	1,652	$636
11	Selling Costs		$156,000		$94
12	General & Administrative Costs		$540,000		$327
13	**Net Income Before Income Taxes**		$355,319		$215

Figure 8-3. Request for Quality Review.

Dear XXXX:

Your assistance is needed to improve our products and services.

Attached are three alternative report formats. Each is a possible output from the accounting department.

You have been selected from among other possible raters because of your experience and knowledge of XX Company's needs.

Please review each report characteristic carefully and rank them from one to three.

	Report Format Number		
Report Characteristic	1	2	3
Sample Ranking	3 (worst)	1 (best)	2 (median)
Relevance			
Completeness			
Readability			
Clarity			
Overall Impression			

Please write other remarks and comments below. The accounting quality circle will consider all information submitted in revising the report before validation.

because although they are usually not interested in the details of accounting, they are very much interested in better information. Bringing these customers into the process of developing the forms and content of information they use will make the reports containing that information more valuable. It will allow the accounting function to demonstrate that delayed data including arbitrary cost assignments can be improved with customer involvement. Letting these customers tell us what they need and want, then responding in a total quality way will add value to the company as a whole and to the accounting function in particular.

DEPARTMENT MANAGERS ARE PERFORMANCE ORIENTED

Department managers are usually placed just below the top management team on organization charts. These managers work at the level where the

actual work for which they are responsible is done by others, and someone more powerful in the organization holds them accountable. It is a
highly stressful position and, consequently, department managers need to
be very performance oriented. Such middle managers are concerned with
how their departments are doing against budget, standards, and prior
periods. Department managers are perhaps our most important cost
accounting customers, in terms of their ability to affect organizational
performance based on accounting information. Quick reporting and accuracy are critical.

One or two non-accounting managers are likely to be involved in the
accounting department-level quality circle as representatives of internal
customers. We should choose carefully when recruiting line department
representatives for the accounting quality circle. We want members who
are willing to serve, who are capable of meaningful contributions, and who
are esteemed by their colleagues. Their active participation is valuable in
improving accounting products and essential in lending credibility to new
products and improvements. A selection technique that is occasionally
used is to recruit those who complain most about accounting, if their complaints are real and worthy of attention.

Department managers' involvement doesn't stop with accounting quality circles, though. Even those who are not actual members of an
accounting quality circle can be surveyed as to the quality of the accounting products they receive. In addition, for major action team projects, like
budget designs or due dates for cost reporting, department managers and
some of their first-line supervisors can be recruited as action team members. Managers who are not members of accounting quality circles are
also useful participants in formal validation of report characteristics, as
described earlier. For example, when a new report has been designed or
an old one altered in response to customers' desires, we will want to
know whether we have "hit the target." Department managers who are not
part of the accounting quality circle can be used to validate the value of
the new information. Any of the techniques mentioned earlier can be
used (e.g., focus groups or surveys).

Turning the situation around, accountants can participate in the quality
circles and action teams of other departments. Since the number of departments in most companies is limited, it should be possible to have a member
of the accounting department on each department's quality circle. Just as
managers should be carefully selected for the accounting circle(s), accountants should be carefully chosen for operating and staff department circles.
Those selected will of course require training in total quality techniques, but
will also have to be proficient accountants who can contribute to the needs
of the department to which they are assigned. They cannot take the narrow

view of their own jobs, but must be aware of all the capabilities of their company's accounting system. These capabilities serve operating managers in both of the typical accounting department's functions, performing administrative services such as disbursements and measuring unit performance through reports and statements. To contribute in both functional areas, accountants who have worked in only one area may require added training. Such training is a good idea anyway, to better integrate the accounting department and improve its workers' capabilities, as discussed in the preceding chapter.

When accountants serve on circles in other departments, they must also have a clear picture of their ability to commit the accounting department. A good rule is that some number of hours of the circle member's own time, say five hours a week, can be committed without requiring approval. If other members of the accounting department will have to commit time, if a substantive change in procedures or reports is wanted, or if the involved accountant needs more time than the amount allowed, the accountant should be required to seek approval.

Working together on improving their organization's processes and products will bring the operating departments and accountants into a cooperative and understanding relationship that was seldom seen before the total quality movement. Department managers are in a key position to facilitate this cooperation and understanding. With their appreciation and awareness of accounting's potential, the accounting function can take its proper place on the overall company team.

Involving department managers in these ways helps ensure that they, and all middle managers, will be pleased with the accounting products they receive. They can help us assess the value of our products' attributes and find ways to produce them more efficiently. Their inclusion in the TQM process within our accounting function also ensures credibility for the changes that are made as our quality circles and action teams work on cost accounting issues. Accountants' inclusion on department quality circles and action teams completes the integration of operations with the accounting department's dual functions of administrative service and performance measurement.

FIRST-LINE SUPERVISORS—THE HOUR-BY-HOUR MANAGERS

Many industrial accountants have observed that shop and field supervisors use accounting reports primarily to stay out of trouble when their bosses ask difficult questions. Supervisors often do not apply accounting information to their daily management actions.

The term *daily management actions* is key to understanding the first-line supervisor's position in most organizations. First-line supervisors usually do not hire their workers. They do not select their equipment. They do not assign or lay out their work areas. They do not select the material their workers use or determine the schedule and priorities. The traditional supervisor's lack of influence is changing rapidly in total quality organizations, but when TQM is newly inaugurated, it will still be so. This lack of power over resources and task assignments will, in any event, have shaped the management habits of the supervisors. They have learned to use accounting data only to keep the boss quiet; they actually manage by more immediate data. The usual criticism is that the accounting data is too late and includes arbitrary cost assignments not directly tied to costs through traceable causal links.

The criticism of timeliness can be addressed in two ways, one conventional and one at the edge of readily usable technology. The conventional approach is to achieve a faster close of the books at the end of each accounting period. Information on each period that is available by the fifth day of the following period is a typical and achievable target. Some companies have achieved two-day closes.

The second approach gives even quicker access to data. It is to implement a distributed data processing system, with terminals in each shop. The terminal can be used for transactions in production control and cost accounting information as work proceeds. Job tickets and time cards need no longer be sent in to a central group for data entry. The data is entered right in the shop, often through bar codes on workers' badges and on each item, batch, or service order being processed. In services, portable transactors are sometimes used, like those used by UPS and Federal Express couriers. A terminal can also be used for daily updates on the previous day's operations, or even used real-time to produce information with no delay at all if programming permits continuous updating as data is entered.

The second criticism, that of irrelevance due to arbitrary cost assignments, has been addressed by direct costing. Direct costing is far more relevant for economically "right" decisions than absorption costing. The advantages of direct costing are even more powerful in first-line supervision, since so many costs are fixed from the supervisor's viewpoint.

More recently, the development of activity-based costing (ABC) in the mid to late 1980s has permitted tracing "upstream" service costs to organizational units that use internal services. ABC arose from some of the first TQM implementations as an early product of TQM's customer-focused approach to the cost accounting problems of relevance, utility, and timeliness. After considerable attention in professional literature and much practical development, ABC has become a valuable addition to the "tool kit" available to meet supervisors' need for relevant information.

Activity-based costing and other tools can be applied through the total quality management process to make accounting reports useful in daily management. There are two major areas for improvement: quality and accuracy of data that comes from the shops and utility of the accounting reports themselves. One calls for action at the work site, the other for action in the accounting process. Since supervisors are both data suppliers and customers for the resulting reports, their participation is crucial to improvement. It's a cooperative effort; better cost assignment requires changes on both sides.

For example, if your company has a cost analysis section in the accounting department, and its quality circle includes one or two first-line supervisors, each new improvement opportunity will be sure to address their need for information that they can understand quickly, that measures the performance factors they can best control, and that is provided soon enough to act while a problem is small and within statistical control limits.

While representatives of first-line supervision are needed on permanent quality circles, they should be included on action teams as well. Certainly, any action team working on data-gathering methods or on shop floor reports needs representatives from the levels where the work is actually done and where the data describing the work originates.

Even ideal accounting procedures and data accessibility will be useless, though, if the data that originates on the shop floor is error ridden. Worse, intentional data manipulation is more common than we generally admit. A military aviators' saying applies here: "Fly what you can and log what you need." In aviation's early days, aviators would do what circumstances allowed, but report what would make life easier in dealing with administrative structures and bosses. First-line supervisors do this too. I recall a case where the foreman kept everyone's time cards. He assigned the work, but reported hours on each job to meet standards. If he really used his accounting reports he would care about the accuracy of this data, but for him "boss pressures" were more important. (This particular occurrence would have been less likely if actual costs were reported without standards, as some advocate. As it happens, the standards were later dropped when TQM was implemented in the shop in question.)

The previous suggestion of real-time data entry through distributed data processing in each work location can also reduce errors. Data must be entered as events occur, so it is harder to save transactions until they can be manipulated in concert with others. Further, the training that must accompany both TQM and distributed data processing can teach a supervisor to value accurate information rather than simply trying to avoid recriminations. In any case, the pressure of reprimands should be greatly reduced by TQM's emphasis on problem-solving instead of blaming. When "discussions with the boss" occur, manipulating data will be a far worse "crime" than any honest misjudgment in operations.

With TQM, boss pressures are less important since the TQM effort is to identify what really happened based on quantifiable data. The question is not "Who can we blame?" but "What can we do?" As accountants we contribute to answering "What happened?" and "What can we do?" by providing the most critical information quickly. Only cost reporting's direct customers, the first-line supervisors, can tell us what aspects of our products are worth the cost and time invested in producing them and only they can ensure the accuracy of the data used.

Consequently, a liaison is necessary between accounting and production quality circles. Interlocking quality circle membership provides the needed liaison. When shop representatives share information about accounting capabilities with quality circles in their parent departments and bring user perspectives to accounting efforts, we begin to see results in both accounting effectiveness and operating efficiency.

WORKERS AS CONTRIBUTORS AND AS CUSTOMERS

The picture would not be complete if we left the subject of internal customers and cooperation without mentioning the production and staff workers who depend on the accounting department. Of course, everyone in the organization depends on accounting for payroll and, in many small and mid-sized companies, for employee benefits administration as well. For these "retail customers" we want the time spent dealing with the accounting department to be as pleasant as possible. Ideally, there will be no problems, but everyone's life unfolds differently, and employees seem to have problems no one has ever thought of before. When these things happen, there are often payroll, vacation, leave, or benefits implications that require contact with the accounting department.

To see how to handle our retail customers, we can look at traditional retailers and sales organizations. We can also look at organizations that regularly deal with people under stress and in an unfamiliar environment. Was your last visit to the dentist or doctor eased by the office staff? If it was, how did they do it? There are special courses for those who work in such offices which tell them how to give patients as pleasant an experience as circumstances permit. Patience, understanding, and an explanation of what will be done and what to expect is always reassuring. A comfortable waiting area and carefully chosen colors are also helpful.

Making employees' dealings with the accounting department as pleasant as possible has implications for company-wide teamwork and for employee loyalty. More selfishly, it will enhance the department's reputation among supervisors and managers. When entry-level associates become managers themselves, they will be well disposed toward the accounting functions and ready to work together toward common goals.

Another area in which line and staff workers are accounting customers arises in *open accounting* situations. Open accounting will be discussed in the next chapter. In open accounting, performance reports are released to all workers in each cost center, so they can see how their section is doing. In these cases, the workers are "retail buyers" of the reports, of course, but they are also suppliers of the data, leading to a mutual relationship. A joint worker-supervisor-accounting action team is a good way to design such reports. Such a team will also allow participating workers to discover for themselves the importance of accurate, timely data entry at the "touch labor" level.

A total quality organization seeks to serve all its customers effectively. One of the means used to do so is empowering workers to make improvements in products and processes. Accounting departments contribute to workers' ability to make such improvements by providing pleasant, prompt, personal service in payroll and allied functions and by providing accurate information to assess improvements that are proposed in workers' daily jobs. Finally, in open accounting situations, line workers are direct customers of the reporting function too.

THE COMPANY'S CUSTOMERS AS ACCOUNTING CUSTOMERS

Although we usually think of customers for accounting information as being inside our organizations, there are outside customers as well. Some of these are government agencies that regulate certain activities, but our company's "real" customers are also beneficiaries of the accounting processes of collecting, classifying, summarizing, and analyzing information.

Consumers

If we're in a consumer goods company, we may think that the grocery store customer can't help our cost accounting. And although she cannot do so directly, she can help indirectly. Out marketing department is constantly conducting research into consumer preferences. Once we know which features of our company's products are valued, we can focus our cost reporting on those features. Then production can look for better, cheaper ways to please the customer while marketing sets prices so the customer pays for the features most valued rather than for those that aren't worth the cost. The same arguments for using market research data apply to non-consumer goods companies too, of course. The important point is that accounting information must be blended with marketing data to tell us where product improvement efforts will be most beneficial to the customer. One is a source of cost information and the other is a source of value information. Together they can allow Pareto analysis, whether formal or informal, to direct resources most productively.

Other Businesses as Customers

While household consumers can contribute indirectly to better accounting, commercial customers offer more direct opportunities. Like household consumers, their preferences about the items they buy from our company can tell us what product features should be objects of cost attention. In addition, business customers are likely to be large-volume buyers with whom we have lasting relationships. Such customers are often glad to participate in improving the operations of their vendors, especially if both parties are TQM practitioners. The opportunity to participate in the vendor certification program of a total quality customer should not be missed. Although it may seem difficult at times, it will yield better results for all our customers and better market position for the firm.

We can also apply some of the market research techniques we discussed in part 1, such as Delphi or focus groups, or we can ask customer representatives to join action teams. Customer representation on action teams is helpful in cases where billing or other customer interfaces are involved, of course, but also in all systems development work where customer integration is advancing through supplier partnerships. Improvements in delivery, billing, and receiving payment are possible in the accounting area, as well as improvements in design and delivery by production areas of the company.

Another opportunity to involve our company's customers in our accounting TQM process is to review the customers' internal accounting methods. This can be done effectively and in a structured manner through benchmarking or best-practices studies. These studies are effective in establishing a closer acquaintance with the company's customers and in integrating their procedures with ours. Advantages can be especially pronounced where the customer is a downstream processor of our company's products.

Cost-Plus Contracts

For many companies, customers have little direct involvement with the cost accounting methods used internally, but there is a case where they do, and a close involvement at that. That case is cost-plus contracts. In a cost-plus contract, common in government procurement and certain custom development industries, the costs incurred in a supplier firm are passed on to the customer, with a stated markup, as the price of the service or item produced. Thus, the supplier's costs transfer directly to become the customer's costs. The cost accounting methods used internally thereby determine the customer's costs. For this reason, cost accounting principles are often recited in the contracts, or incorporated by reference to such standards as the Department of Defense's Cost Accounting Standards Board.

Not only are buyers of the company's products accounting customers in the sense that they are affected by the results of internal accounting methods, but they are also direct consumers of data in that they usually have audit privileges under cost-plus contracts. When contract auditors use our internal records and information to analyze their companies' product costs, they are looking for compliance with the contract, of course, but also for opportunities to improve their specifications for more cost-effective purchasing on their part. Keeping records that combine sound economic theory with contract requirements will allow such analysis by our company's customers and by ourselves.

An effective way to meet customers' needs for such information is to include them in the development of cost accounting methods and products. It offers added benefits by demonstrating our desire to meet customer needs, thereby aiding sales. A good way to get such involvement is to include them in action teams and quality circles where feasible. Considerations in deciding whether to invite customer representatives for such meetings include the need to safeguard our own company's proprietary information and any data we might have that is proprietary to other customers. Still, where it can be done and fits the situation, customer representatives are useful members of quality circles and action teams.

Conclusion

Although it seems unlikely at first glance and although it won't be the first step in accounting TQM implementation, there is opportunity for our companies' ultimate customers to assist in improving our accounting products. They can do so through market research that tells us which product features most deserve cost accounting emphasis and through direct participation where processes in two companies interface.

THE GOVERNMENT AS AN ACCOUNTING INFORMATION CUSTOMER

Not all customers for accounting information have commercial links to our organizations. Some are federal or state agencies to which certain regulated industries must report. All firms report to the Internal Revenue Service and many to the Securities and Exchange Commission as well. These agencies are customers of an enterprise's accounting department just as internal users are.

The next points may be hard to swallow if you're used to an adversarial relationship with government agencies. However, there can be benefits to regulatory participation in a quality management effort. If you are a federal supplier, you are aware of the current emphasis on TQM; this is a chance to get out in front of your company's federal customer rather than being forced into compliance. Remember too that federal agencies have some discretion in choosing suppliers; it isn't all just price.

If you're working in a regulated utility, there is less of a sales advantage to your company, but TQM still offers an opportunity to demonstrate to the rate authority that you are seeking to improve service and that any profit increases need not come at the customers' expense.

Convincing regulators that total quality initiatives will be to the advantage of the groups served is not hard in today's climate, where TQM is widely recognized even though it is not yet widely practiced. Groups served can be the governments themselves for procurement actions, consumers for regulated utilities, or third parties where medical or similar services are contracted by governments on behalf of certain classes of citizens in need of services. In the case of third party beneficiaries, tenant councils or patient representatives are almost certain to be approved by regulators. Since conflicts are less likely where the government is acting for another's benefit, regulatory participation on accounting action teams is possible and may be approved.

For other situations, government procurement agents are likely to see a conflict in participating in the development of processes that report data to them. They may think of it as "auditing their own work" when they receive reports prepared by processes they helped design. Such conflicts do not really exist, of course, since the report content has already been prescribed. If this objection arises, the participation can often be obtained by calling it an *assist visit* or a *quality assurance measure* rather than a reporting change effort.

Another possibility is that regulatory reports can be altered to share data and preparation processes with internal reports. For example, the IRS accepts data in many forms, including electronic transmission. If you've used a commercial tax preparation package, you have probably noticed that the forms the program prints are similar, but not identical to the "official" forms at the post office. They have been approved by the IRS as substitutes, however. Just as it is possible to get Private Letter Rulings on tax treatment of certain items, it is possible to get report formats approved. The same thing may be possible with your local and state agencies.

As an example of using TQM procedures to meet IRS requirements, ALCOA used an action team to improve its response during a coordinated examination. ALCOA was subject to the IRS's Coordinated Examination Program, where IRS agents enter large companies and audit two or three years' returns at a time. Part of this procedure is that the IRS sends Information Document Requests (IDR), which give the company 30 days to respond. Failure to make the deadline has consequences for the IRS agents' perception of cooperation, of course, and their willingness to grant extensions and to accept company representations. It also allows the agents to raise added issues or develop new approaches as they seek information in other ways when a response to an IDR is not on time. ALCOA established an action team that developed eight improvement possibilities for controlling the response process, assigning responsibility, and documenting the outcomes for future use.

Establishing teams of internal users, accountants, and representatives of regulatory agencies can lead to efficiencies as reports are designed to serve dual purposes. Where the reports must differ, the data collection can often be consolidated to avoid duplicate effort. Agencies frequently have discretion to make changes in their requirements and will do so if they see a reason.

Even if we want them to participate, can we persuade representatives of regulatory agencies to join our quality circles and action teams? It sounds impossible, but recall that defense contractors often have Department of Defense representatives in their plants. These representatives are good candidates for quality circle membership, if safeguards are provided so they are clearly not participating in management of the enterprise, but are instead improving performance for the customer's benefit.

Action teams aren't the only way these agencies can participate, either, although they have been stressed in the discussion so far. A process something like market research is also possible, wherein small teams can interview regulatory agency representatives for viewpoints and suggestions on how to be more responsive to public needs. Such a procedure can also give the regulator an appreciation of the company's situation as it tries to meet the demands placed on it.

Members of quality circles and action teams whose projects will benefit from regulators' input can delegate members to interview those who receive and use their reports. (Be sure to include tax or legal counsel in planning such interviews, however, since the best workers may not always be aware of regulatory issues underlying the information they deal with in their team projects.) Understanding the uses of information at agencies that receive reports will allow better action team outcomes in both product and process. It will also ensure that the team doesn't go off in a direction that leads to later repercussions and even penalties. An agency is likely to be so impressed by the cooperation of an "information supplier" from among its regulated population that other matters become smoother as well; the customer relations value of TQM should not be overlooked in this area any more than in the case of "real customers."

If these agencies are surveyed in the design of accounting products, can we be more effective operationally? Maybe, maybe not. Can we avoid regulatory wrangles? Probably, since our reports reflect the information needed by regulators. Will we be better suppliers to our direct customers, our fellow citizens? Apparently the voters think so, because they set up these regulatory agencies through the political process.

In summary, regulatory authorities are established to look after the public interest, which is also our interest. In public utilities and defense suppliers especially, they are our ultimate customers' representatives. We can get along better in serving all our customers if we find a way to work together in balancing everyone's needs. Since regulatory authorities use the products of our accounting processes, they may have ideas that can improve those products. Two ways to get those ideas are through action team participation where feasible or less formal discussion where direct participation is ruled out.

9

WHEN THE ACCOUNTING DEPARTMENT IS THE CUSTOMER

Just as the customers of the accounting function need quality products delivered in timely fashion, accountants need to receive quality products in a timely fashion from suppliers. Since late information is not as useful to our customers as recent, rapidly delivered information, late data to accounting results in lower-quality accounting products. They may be inherently good, but their lateness decreases their usefulness. Another attribute that contributes to the quality of accounting products is accuracy, meaning that the information conveyed must reflect the actual events in the operating functions of the business.

Both timeliness and accuracy depend in part on the internal processes of accounting to work rapidly and correctly, but they also depend on outsiders to provide the data that is needed, and to provide it promptly. In this case, our customer is also often our supplier; the operating shops that use classified and summarized accounting information also provide the data that is used to generate it.

We have already mentioned the ability of both operating departments and the accounting function to share membership on quality circles and action teams that deal with cross-functional issues. Interlocking memberships provide representation that ensures that the needs of the customer are met, and met in both directions. They also ensure that when a customer, either an operating department for information or the accounting department for data, devises an apparent improvement that calls for a change by the other, the change is workable. It would do no good to devise an ideal process if the raw material were unavailable.

To get useful, timely data from operating departments is often a difficult task. Line operators can always find some reason why they "had to solve the problem" and leave the paperwork for later. A first response to this situation is to note that in a total quality company, there will be fewer and fewer problems that need high-pressure, emergency solutions. A second response is that the data-gathering actions required of operating personnel should be as automatic as possible, and so ingrained into the service or production process that it is easier to produce the data than not. In fact, it is a basic principle of any process design that to get compliance, the procedure should be easier to do right than to do wrong. This is especially true when working with operations personnel as suppliers of data because of their frequent aversion to paperwork and the press of events when they must serve the company's ultimate customers.

An example of simplifying the data-gathering process occurred in a large manufacturing facility when it switched much of its processing to bar code data entry. Previously, each operator received a *job sheet* in a batch of material for processing. The operator was required to transfer information such as the job number, the quantity (often stopping to count parts), and the procedure to be performed to a *work ticket*. When the operation was finished, the work ticket was completed with hours spent and any tools, taps, or dies also recorded. The work ticket was sent to production control offices for data entry. Any interruption in the job, such as diverting work effort to a higher priority task, might or might not be recorded, depending on the amount of rush imposed on a worker and his conscientious or lackadaisical attitude toward paperwork. In addition, there were opportunities for error at each copying step.

With bar coding, the facility was able to instantly record a job process's beginning, the worker involved, and any tool or material issues by scanning codes on workers' badges, parts containers, and material tags. The built-in computer clock kept hours, and if a worker clocked onto a rush job, time was automatically suspended on the basic job. If a worker failed to clock back onto a suspended job, the starting of the next operation recorded the previous operation as complete. Audit routines (such as matching operations' required skills to employees and matching material issues to stock on hand and to bills of material) and check digits in identifying numbers eliminated almost all errors.

The point of the example is that for a worker to do his job, he had only a few simple bar scans to accomplish rather than copying many digits of information onto paper. Further, there was no paper to lose. The automated check routines ensured that material issues were restricted to jobs the worker was actually recorded as working on. Consequently, it was much easier to "do the right thing" than to ignore or circumvent the data entry process. The data was more timely as well.

We can conclude that when working with our internal data suppliers, we should make their jobs as simple and error-free as possible. Interlocking quality circle and action team membership helps ensure that we ask only for what is possible, and designing processes with the user in mind will provide more accurate and timely input while relieving operating personnel of much of the paperwork burden they often blame on their accounting departments.

THE DATA PROCESSING DEPARTMENT AS A SUPPLIER

In the same way that an organization forms partnerships with its outside suppliers, the accounting department can form partnerships with internal suppliers. We usually can't threaten to seek other vendors, although some companies have gone that far, but we can use supplier departments' implementation of total quality management as a positive force in forging beneficial relationships. If the TQM implementation is proceeding evenly throughout the company, it should reach working levels in supplier departments at about the same time it reaches working levels in accounting.

The staff section that most affects accounting operations is the data processing department. Data processing departments in industry are at differing stages of development. In the early days of large computer rooms with special climate controls, data processing was something like magic. No one else was ordinarily allowed to know what went on there. Later, with personal computers, many workers broke their dependence on data processing departments and avoided the need for programming requests and attendant delays. Instead, while continuing to use primary applications on mainframe computers, they began to do their analysis on PCs using packaged programs such as Visicalc™, dBASE™, and successor programs like Lotus 1-2-3™, Excel™, and Access™. As the data processing department saw its grip slipping, it tried to get the PCs under its control, but was not entirely successful. Now workers could use computers too, so with the magic gone, data processing departments were forced to become more customer oriented. Today, even mainframes are being displaced in all but the largest companies; PC networks are taking their place. Various companies are at different stages in this process of data processing development. Each will presumably settle on a set of internal rules that works in its particular culture and environment.

Wherever your company may be today, or wherever it may be going in its data processing development, the data processing department is probably a supplier to accounting functions. In small companies the accounting department may also be the data processing department, maintaining the local network and PCs. In such cases, it can helpful to view the functions separately, seeing the accounting department as its own customer for data processing services.

As in other relationships in an organization where one department's work affects another, interlocking representation on quality circles and action teams is the total quality management imperative. A highly successful example of such integration occurred in a firm that was moving into TQM and distributed data processing at the same time. Rather than having the data processing department collect all user requests and present them with "the solution," the company formed an action team with representatives of user departments like production control and accounting added to the data processing and maintenance professionals. The result was PC-based computing at the user level where each PC was on a network and included terminal emulation software.

In this way, mainframe applications were accessible along with local analysis capability. The cost of separate terminals and PCs was avoided. Three levels of PC software were chosen: an integrated package (like Lotusworks™ or Works for Windows™) to provide multiple capabilities for most users, a second layer of programs that were supported by the data processing department (like Lotus 1-2-3™, WordPerfect™, and dBASE™) for requirements where the integrated package was too limited, and a custom search for specialized applications where none of the standard programs would do what the user needed. The type of PC, the terminal emulation programs, and the PC applications were all selected by the action team, with input from a survey of users in affected departments.

In another case in a smaller company, an action team was formed to select a new accounting and reporting package for use on a local area network. Again, representatives of operating and administrative departments were included in the selection process. The result was that although no packaged program exactly fits most businesses, the team was able to recognize that fact. Seeing that the company was growing rapidly and changing quickly, they chose the most adaptable program from those they examined, and have been able to meet most of their needs with very little off-line analysis.

From earlier discussions of TQM and accounting, and from these examples, we see that supplier partnerships with the data processing department assure that accountants as customers receive the data processing tools needed to do their jobs. Including data processing professionals in accounting circles and teams further ensures that the capabilities of the data processing department are considered when devising accounting improvements. It also affords opportunity for the "accounting story" to be carried back to the work sections of the data processing department, leading to better integration and teamwork for all.

THE PERSONNEL DEPARTMENT AS A SUPPLIER

Accounting departments use data processing continuously, but use the personnel department less often. Each personnel department action is correspondingly more important, though, since it is much harder to reverse a poor personnel assignment than a poor data input or programming decision. The cost is likely to be higher as well. Besides hiring and assignments, personnel departments are involved in personnel maintenance functions, such as regular reviews, benefits, counseling, and training.

It is probably less important to include an accounting representative on personnel quality circles than on data processing quality circles since accounting demands on the personnel department are not unique. Accounting department needs will probably be adequately addressed by any staff department's representative. Of course, this doesn't mean such representation should be avoided, but only indicates where it will typically fall in priority when there are competing demands. If a controller wants representation, circles and teams that deal with employee benefits are good choices, since benefits often have payroll processing and cost implications. Of the other areas usually included in personnel departments, training is most likely to affect accounting operations, since the training needed by accountants is likely to be technical in nature. Certified accountants (CIAs, CMAs, and CPAs) will also need continuing education to maintain their certificates, and consequently should have their needs addressed by the training section of the personnel department. Therefore, representation on the training quality circle should be considered. A certified individual is a good candidate.

We have seen that the personnel department is both a supplier and a customer of the accounting department, but primarily a supplier. The most critical of its services are in hiring and assignment and in training. In the employee benefits area, cooperation between the departments is helpful to serve their mutual customers. For these reasons, some cross-representation on quality circles and action teams is helpful. While it should be regular, it need not be intensive. Just as the idea of external supplier relationships is to become so confident of one another that inspection is eliminated, we should work together so that what we ask for is clear, and so that we can be sure of getting what we really need from the personnel department. This calls for developing confidence and trust in one another and in our processes through shared knowledge, cooperation, and personal acquaintance. As we've seen, total quality organizations offer such opportunities as part of their normal management processes.

OTHER INTERNAL SUPPLIERS

Other internal service functions provide the physical needs of the accounting department. These functions are material, administrative services, office services, and plant services. These departments may be structured differently in different companies so that not all titles are used. Every company, however, will have functional departments that provide supplies, furnishings, building maintenance, equipment maintenance, printing, and similar materials and services to sustain the accounting department.

The internal service departments that supply the accounting department also use accounting products, of course, like any other functional department. It would be reasonable, therefore, to expect that each would be represented on the others' quality circles and action teams, in order to ensure that the products and services provided are of the kinds and quality needed.

We must recognize that every organization has many internal customer relationships, but that its main purpose is to serve its ultimate, outside customers. Outside customers' interests should be foremost in the organization's improvement efforts, and so those departments whose products lead directly to the product or service that goes to the ultimate customer will receive priority attention in the improvement process.

To give the ultimate customers the priority they deserve, the functional departments who serve them most directly will be heavily represented on accounting department circles and teams, and that unfortunately leaves only limited room for internal service department representatives. The priorities of other internal service functions are also properly focused on work that most affects the ultimate customers' value received, and consequently will have limited space in their circles and teams for accounting representation. Fortunately, internal customers often use similar outputs and one or a few can represent all.

Although cross-membership on quality circles is limited by available numbers and time, action teams also offer an opportunity to share involvement. Action team members are selected for their ability to contribute to the specific improvement opportunity that the team is chartered for. Permanent quality circles, on the other hand, review many improvement opportunities and must be constituted to address them all. Therefore, these circles will have a more diverse membership. Remember, not every internal service department can fit in every quality circle.

Since not all internal service functions can be represented in each others' quality circles, and since each should be represented somewhere, we must coordinate quality circle assignments. All internal services should be represented somewhere in the accounting department's quality circles. Similarly, accountants should be included somewhere in other internal service circles.

Links like these ensure that internal services are represented in each others' quality circles while not overshadowing the needs of the "real production" departments. After all, the production departments are the ones that directly serve the organization's ultimate customers, and therefore must receive priority in a customer-focused company. Limited, well-chosen links also ensure that internal service departments, which are smaller than production departments, are not over-taxed.

WORKING WITH OUTSIDE SERVICES AS SUPPLIERS

Many companies, especially large ones, do nearly everything internally. Smaller companies often use outside services. Even larger companies increasingly are using outside specialists for functions that used to be done internally. Ross Perot built EDS by taking over data processing departments. EDS will buy a company's entire computer suite, hire its employees, and operate it on a negotiated fee-for-service structure. More commonly, a payroll and tax filing service is used to prepare paychecks for a company.

Outside services like these make sense because they are specialists in what they do, just as our companies specialize in their own areas of work. If our customers did everything for themselves, we would have no purpose! Instead, each organization balances its resources, market opportunities, and other factors to determine how much management attention is available and how much it wants to hire specialty service companies to do its service and support work. Besides data processing and payroll service, which affect accounting directly, janitorial service, maintenance, and cafeterias are often contracted out.

In addition to continuing relationships like those mentioned, companies often use outside services as occasional supplements to internal functions. Employment agencies, engineering firms, law firms, and equipment repair shops may handle overflow work or special assignments even where an organization has internal capability. Finally, temporary help agencies often provide trained workers within our departments.

An accounting department must deal with these suppliers in seeing that contracts are administered well and that payments are made promptly and in accordance with agreed terms. In some cases, however, the relationship goes beyond that.

Cases of deeper involvement are those where accounting departments use the services directly in producing accounting products. These are primarily those mentioned earlier, payroll and data processing services. In these cases, we may want to have representatives of these services on our internal quality circles. If they are not invited to join at the beginning, it may be considered for a later, more fully developed stage of total quality implementation. More likely, representatives of such outside suppliers will be invited to join quality circles only if their work is actually performed on our site. Other factors to consider are the degree to which we are buying a standard service sold to other customers or buying a special, tailored service unique to our company. Typically, a data processing management company might have representatives on our quality circles, while a payroll processing service would not.

It is also possible that outside service companies are themselves total quality organizations. If they were selected after the total quality implementation began in our own company, they were probably selected partly for that reason. In these cases, we can expect to be involved in their customer-focused programs, perhaps by serving on quality circles or customer councils. We can also expect to receive the same kinds of evidence of quality that we provide to our customers. They should have statistical process control charts, where feasible, and scheduled quality audits. Such suppliers should also know their cost of quality.

Many companies regard such information as secret, and will not share it. In forging supplier partnerships, such secretiveness creates obstacles to cooperation and trust. A more open relationship can be expected when dealing with total quality suppliers.

In other cases, outside services do not become part of the products that accounting gives to its customers. With janitorial services, temporary help, and employment agencies the accounting department is one customer among others within an organization. In these cases, there is no specific reason for accountants to seek representation on quality circles. Although members of the accounting department may certainly serve as representatives of customer departments, they will not represent accounting specifically, but will act for all similarly situated customers.

Given the distinction between outside services that directly affect accounting products and those for which accounting is just one customer among others, how do we deal with those who are essential parts of our services?

The answer is that we deal with them just as any total quality firm deals with its suppliers, by establishing partnerships. These include features previously listed, such as statistical control. Partnerships also include mutual visits to exchange information on how each company works internally, so that materials, services, and the products made with them can be suited to one another. Inputs, processes, and products can be modified so that the most value-effective processes evolve as we apply the Shewhart Cycle of continuous improvement.

In summary, accountants should seek closest involvement with external service firms that most affect the accounting processes and products. The primary elements of total quality management, which are customer focus, participation, and data-driven decisions, can be effected by forging partnerships with these suppliers. In this way, we can enjoy a confident relationship and superior inputs to our processes. We can resolve issues that interfere with the quality accounting work we want to provide and we can please our customers within and outside our organizations.

WORKING WITH SUPPLIERS

In the last section, we discussed how a total quality accounting function can deal successfully with outside services. Although we don't think of accounting as a big material consumer, the design of the material that accountants use is important to their efficiency at work.

Accounting is not called "paperwork" for nothing. It uses enormous amounts of prescribed forms. These forms were on paper until recent years when computer screens took over. But the principles are the same: a form, whether on paper or on screen, must be complete, simple, and logical. It must be self-explanatory. It must relate to the events it records. It must be so structured that it fits into the surrounding processes, and is easier to use correctly than to use wrongly. It must also be more convenient to use a form and the procedure of which it is a part than it is to endure the natural consequences of not using it or of using it correctly. Note that I didn't say "the consequences," but "the *natural* consequences." Total quality organizations try to avoid artificial consequences to compel compliance; instead, they aim for natural and simple procedures that become part of the main task whose data they record.

As an example, consider a form that is nearly ideal for the company's purpose, but needs one more bit of data. We can instruct everyone who uses the form to "note the added information on the margin at item 6." If we do this, we must train all of its users—another cost. Worse, we must correct all the cases where the added information is left out, or we must wonder whether it is perhaps not applicable to the situation in each case. Without the reminder of a specific place for information, we can be sure it will be forgotten in many cases. The cost of correction is high if the omission is caught, requiring going back to the originator, who may be in another location altogether. The cost can be higher still if an omission is not caught and an erroneous invoice is sent, if a payment or paycheck is in error, if profitable sales are lost or unprofitable ones made, or if false data is given to operating managers. Sometimes, the cost may never be known.

Another problem arises if there are punishments for incorrect use. If a worker is berated, he will typically become resentful, and all his work will be affected. Even if he complies, malicious compliance is possible where a worker says, "If that's what they want, I'll do it, even where I know it won't work." The enforced procedure is likely to be ignored at the first opportunity.

To avoid problems like this, we need a collegial process for deriving specifications. Certainly, the purchasing department should be involved because they must deal with vendors and execute buys. The material or office services departments must be involved since they will be responsible for safekeeping, issue, and stock levels of forms and supplies. The chief participants in forms and office material specification, though, must be the primary users, to ensure that the items purchased are what they need and neither more nor less.

A good way to do this is to establish a quality circle that is not department-specific for procedures and forms. It might be sponsored by purchasing, office services, administration, or even accounting. Its members are drawn from all affected departments. If available, an industrial engineer can be a helpful member. Where operations are sufficiently uniform in a firm, the operations department should be represented too. Where operations are so varied that one or two representatives could not address most issues, it might be necessary to accommodate their needs on a case-by-case basis. Where a procedure affects those not part of the circle, they may be invited to join temporarily, or an action team may be formed.

Each company must find the structure that best fits its variety of business, level of complexity, and working style. Whatever form it takes and whatever it may be called, a circle, board, or committee can ensure total quality results that are customer focused, participative, and data driven. Forms, screens, and procedures can fit the work and the workers rather than the other way around. It will be easy and natural to do the required information gathering and communication rather than difficult and awkward. The compliance and accuracy rates will increase markedly with reduced costs.

THE PAPERWORK PART OF ACQUISITION

We usually think of our company's suppliers as providing services and products for production activities or for facility-sustaining activities. We forget that those who deliver production material or janitorial services also deliver documents that have to be processed. They have contracts, they render invoices, and they provide proofs of delivery.

These documents represent an instance where working together with our material and service suppliers can yield administrative efficiencies while reducing errors and simplifying everyone's work. In the preceding topics of this chapter, we discussed some ways of working as partners with internal suppliers of accounting data and with outside suppliers of material and services we use in our accounting work. The remaining topic concerns how we can work with those who supply other parts of our organizations, but who also provide materials that accountants need to do their work.

It is not our purpose here to get into a technological discussion of electronic data interchange as a replacement for paper or of computerized systems for internal processing. The basic elements for each transaction remain the same however they may be transmitted and matched. Rather, we want to see that, just as our counterparts who use the material and services that our organizations buy can work with their suppliers on improving purchased items, we can work with those same suppliers on the "paperwork" end.

If our company is at the stage of total quality development that includes vendor certification, we want to be sure to include administrative concerns in that process. These include invoice forms, purchase order information, discounts, and proofs of delivery. Our firm will have many suppliers, and they will often have nearly as many distinct invoice formats. Efficiency and accuracy can be improved if our associates, either data entry or clerical, have only a single format to read. Since vendor certification contemplates long-term partnership relations with suppliers, it is possible to get them to make necessary program changes to produce invoices in a format that is helpful to us, their customer.

Of course, using electronic data interchange requires a uniform format so that the programs at the receiving end can recognize the fields and process incoming data correctly. Since uniform formats are possible for EDI, they can also be obtained on paper, if required. It is very important to remember that the key is to include accounting aspects in the vendor certification program from the beginning, so that administrative concerns are addressed as an integral part of the process. If they are an afterthought, they may not be successfully dealt with, and the accounting department may not be able to provide the kind of consistent, error-free service in paying suppliers that we ask of them in providing the underlying items.

There can be a number of reasons for a particular vendor not being in the vendor certification program: our program may not yet have reached that vendor, the vendor may be a utility where we have no choice in our dealings, or our firm may not have included such a program in its TQM implementation plans, or at least not yet.

When a vendor is not formally part of our TQM implementation, it is still possible to work with him, though, using techniques we have previously covered. Such suppliers can be invited to participate in supplier groups, either ones that meet regularly like a suppliers' council or special ones like focus groups. They can also be invited to join internal quality circles when the volume of business makes them an integral part of a department. This most often occurs where a vendor provides an in-house service, such as a contract data processing service or a contractor for material and inventory management. Any just-in-time vendor is also a good candidate. Their intimate involvement with our company's production processes already makes them a partner, so it is only reasonable to include them in our TQM processes too.

In cases where a supplier is not intimately involved with our company's production processes, but is a more "arm's-length" supplier of standard commercial items or services, he can still be invited to join an action team if one is assigned to work on processes dealing with his invoices or other documents.

In one instance, a company had trouble accounting for project costs when rented equipment was moved from one project to another. The equipment supplier issued a single consolidated invoice listing hundreds of identical items. The customer wanted the invoice broken down by project, so costs could be properly assigned. The supplier knew when a transfer occurred because electronic codes had to be reset by supplier service personnel at each transfer, so the information was available. This supplier, was not a total quality company, and despite promises, never produced the invoices as the customer requested. The result was that customer's clerical personnel had to spend up to three days a month tracing the location of each rented item before paying the invoice. The inefficiency for the customer is obvious, but the supplier's payments were sometimes delayed up to 60 days as the clerk tried to work in the necessary time and waited for confirmations and call-backs from field personnel.

Here's a really interesting case. A company formed an action team to investigate slow payment of vendors. Pareto analysis showed that slow payments were concentrated in a customer group that made small or irregular sales to the company. Large, regularly occurring invoices were usually paid promptly. Pareto analysis further showed that half the suppliers accounted for almost all the late payments, but only a small percentage of dollars spent (an application of the old 80/20 rule). By changing to a purchase order form that included a *payable-through voucher* (a form of check) at the bottom, the vendor was paid in advance, when the order was sent. Controls were established through long-term supplier contracts with random audits. (In other cases, controls could include dollar limits and limitations on the kinds of items and total volume per supplier that could be bought this way.) This eliminated late payments to such vendors. Better terms could be obtained and competition among vendors improved for the company. In the accounting realm, there was only a single matching of the cleared check to the receiving copy of the purchase order, and occasional investigations of cleared vouchers where no receiving copy was turned in by the product or service user. Motorola eliminated 50 percent of vendor paperwork through a procedure of this kind. The Core Supplier program at Procter & Gamble includes provisions for a similar payment scheme.

These examples show that by including administrative and accounting aspects of a supplier relationship at the inception and as an integral part of the total quality process, both our suppliers and our own organizations benefit. The means for including administrative and accounting aspects are those that apply everywhere in total quality management: customer focus, participation, and data-driven decisions. These are addressed by including representatives on quality circles and action teams that deal with vendor relationships. They are also addressed through participation in supplier councils and similar contacts with suppliers, where they exist. It is also possible for the accounting department to initiate contact where a quality circle or action team's work leads to that requirement. Just be sure not to leave out anyone who should be involved, like the purchasing department or users of the items bought from vendors in question; involvement works both ways.

10

ACCOUNTING IMPROVEMENTS

So far, we have looked at total quality management, its philosophy, approaches, and tools. We have examined tools borrowed from other management approaches that are useful in the TQM revolution. We have also examined accounting philosophies, approaches, and tools. We have seen that operating management is not satisfied with typical accounting products, and that there are ways to improve. We have seen that TQM can be applied to accounting products and processes and we've examined where improvement opportunities are most likely to be found. This chapter discusses some concrete areas of financial and accounting operations that are candidates for improvement initiatives. It includes ways to discover improvements and begin their implementation.

IMPROVEMENT OPPORTUNITIES—READABLE REPORTS AND RELEVANT INFORMATION

Line managers often complain that accounting reports are hard to read. The information they really want is obscurely placed and not clearly labeled. As accountants, we realize that they have caused much of this difficulty for themselves. Since each manager has different ideas of what's important, reports end up including everyone's ideas. Another source of cluttered appearance is the need for "backup" or "details." If we present summary information, managers want to know how it was derived, so we frequently include data and calculations on reports whose real point is not in the details, but in the conclusions.

How do these problems come about? Trying to please too many masters comes about, first, because managers begin with different personal management approaches. Second, each has a different base of prior experience and knowledge. Third, each department really is different from every other in some way, and the information needed to manage the departments varies accordingly.

If managers read and interpret information in similar ways, it will be a great help in producing reports that can be read easily by any member of the organization. Uniform interpretation of information requires more or less uniform understanding of the company's operations and of the meaning of financial information. Such uniformity of outlook is achieved through a common base of knowledge that is imparted in training. Recall that training is an essential part of total quality implementation; each manager and each worker must have the knowledge and understanding necessary to do his basic job and to seek continuous improvement in it.

Once training has progressed to include relevant cost interpretation, managers will be equipped to look for and use only information that reflects events they can control and that will actually be affected by the management choices they face. They will be able to recognize which information they receive reflects events outside their control and which information may be useful for each kind of management decision they face.

Uniform understanding of company operations coupled with the knowledge of which information is relevant to managers' work will allow quality circles and action teams to reduce the complexity of reports. As each report is worked on, it will become increasingly relevant to the company's actual operations while leaving out irrelevant or uncontrollable items. Where such items are included "for information purposes," they will be clearly labeled as such and will not distract from the essential work of managers in line functions.

The second source of needless complexity in reporting is the requirement to "show your work." That sounds like grade school mentality because it is. It exists in business for the same reason as it did in grade school—lack of trust. Operating management in many companies has somehow developed a lack of confidence in accounting information, perhaps because of the perception that reported totals include allocations of uncontrollable costs, and that such costs are allocated arbitrarily, with no direct relation to resources actually used in a manager's area of responsibility.

Fortunately, trust in accounting information is built in the same way that uniformity of interpretation is achieved. Training and personal acquaintance are the tools, achieved through the training programs just mentioned and through mutual participation on one another's quality circles and action teams.

While preparing our organizations for better accounting practices and reports through education and shared quality circle and action team membership, it is possible to begin the process of improving the reports themselves. As total quality management becomes our organizations' standard way of doing business, action teams will become the preferred tool for making changes. The changes that are made will be consistent with the users' needs.

After new report formats are designed and the information that will be displayed is defined, some trial copies should be prepared. They will be used first to ensure that what the team had in mind was what the working accountants heard. Second, trial copies will ensure that the data for the new reports is available. Third, it will ensure that the arithmetic is feasible and yields the information that is wanted. Finally, the trial copies can be used to validate the new report formats, by testing them with a group of users that was not directly involved in their development. There's nothing like an outside, detached view to correct any missteps.

As we've seen, such outside views can be obtained through a number of devices. Surveys are one way, but are likely to be pushed aside by the recipients unless presented and collected personally by team members. (When contacting survey recipients personally, team members must be careful not to guide them to say what the members hope to hear.) Focus groups can be good because the focus group members can interact and reach a consensus, or by bouncing ideas off one another they can guide further improvement. Another useful validation technique, where the TQM implementation includes them, is to refer the proposed "more readable" information formats to a quality review board or to a committee of a quality circle that includes members from user departments.

As you can see, the exact techniques chosen to make any improvement are dependent on the nature of each organization, its culture, its structure, its stage of TQM implementation, and who is affected by any particular improvement proposal. Whatever mechanisms work in your situation, readability is one opportunity to improve accounting products and win the appreciation of operating management. Such changes illustrate the desire and ability of the accounting function to "join the team" by contributing to success in any way possible, and to be a cooperator rather than a roadblock to line managers.

OPEN ACCOUNTING

One of the tenets that often goes with conventional financial management is that everything is secret, and only those who need information can have it. The implication is that very few people need comprehensive information on a unit's performance, fewer need information on the total enterprise's operations, and almost no one is allowed to know the overall financial situation. In publicly held companies, it is impossible to hide the quarterly and annual statements, but they are seldom elaborated and hardly ever explained to the workers whose labors are reflected in them.

Total quality management does not try to overwhelm workers with financial data, but it acknowledges that all the associates in a firm want the best for their organization (unless they have been alienated by exclusionary practices and arbitrary management), that everyone needs to feel "in the know," and that our fellow workers at all levels are more intelligent than we usually recognize. TQM recognizes that we all must pull together toward our company's goals, and we can do so only if we know what those goals and strategies are, and if we know how the organization is doing in its efforts.

When we don't know what the goal is, we continue to do our best, but at least some of our abilities are distracted from the main task by trying to guess what the boss wants. Of course, the boss has the same problem with his boss. If circumstances change, we can't adapt our own work to meet the new conditions, because we don't know what we're really trying to achieve, or where we are in our movement toward it.

An example of effort misdirected through ignorance is furnished by my grandfather, an old-fashioned construction company owner. When I was a teenager, he assigned me to cut into a field with a power mower, along a certain direction, about a six-foot swath. He went on to another job, and became preoccupied. When he returned, I had cut all the way across the field! But he wasn't satisfied with the results, though he didn't berate me. It's just that he was looking for a surveyor's marker (called a "man") that he thought was out there somewhere. If he had told me what he was really after, I could have led him right to it, since I had passed it while getting the mower out. And if I knew that he was looking for the "man" as a checkpoint to find the property line and site a fence, even that trouble could have been saved, because the remains of old fence-posts also appeared when we walked the ground.

The point is that workers can meet customers' requirements only when they know what those requirements are and how they fit into the overall purpose. When new circumstances arise, they can seek ways to adapt. But if management reserves all knowledge and authority to itself, only management can make necessary adaptations. Managers can't be everywhere and know everything, so inefficiencies result. Sometimes whole lots of product are ruined, or weeks are spent on computer programs that meet the specifications the programmer got, but that don't serve the actual purpose. The requester didn't know what the programmer would find when looking into actual data file structure, and didn't tell the programmer the real purpose of the request.

Financial measures aren't the only measures, of course, but they are important, and offer some benefits not achieved by other kinds of data. For one thing, financial information is expressed in a standard unit, namely dollars, and therefore equates resources that are not easily compared in pounds or number of items. Also, explaining financial information uniquely conveys management's confidence in the workforce. No other kind of data carries quite the same message of confidence and team spirit.

Some companies are beginning to combat such problems by sharing financial information with their workers. These companies are beginning to practice *open accounting*. They show confidence in the intelligence and good will of their workers and they eliminate unnecessary secrecy. Effort can be directed to productive ends rather than to second-guessing and suspicion.

The kinds of information that are shared are virtually unlimited, since such companies recognize that their competitive advantages lie in their work-force and the quality of their services, not in the secrecy of their financial results. Consequently, they make financial results an open book, with the basic, enterprise-wide financial statements released to the firms' associates first, then to outsiders.

In addition, and perhaps more to the point, each shop, branch, facility, or work unit gets its own financial results. Sometimes they are even presented formally in a monthly session by the supervisor, the plant accountant, or a designated representative of the accounting department. After the prepared briefing, questions can be taken from the work group.

The question-and-answer period gives opportunity to explain cost assignments and thus the causal relationships among cost elements, along with some basic economic concepts. With this education, workers will make more intelligent choices in using resources where trade-offs are possible.

For example, in one shop, workers had the idea that the expensive grease (with special additives) used during assembly should be conserved. When they saw the warranty costs that resulted from saving a little grease, they made a much more intelligent choice. In another case I observed, workers ran their machines hard, then called maintenance when they had problems. When they saw the cost of emergency maintenance, they learned to do preventive maintenance themselves, to operate their equipment within its design limits, and to recognize incipient problems. They were able to stop production before equipment failed, saving both the equipment repairs and the product that might have been unacceptable because of a failing machine.

Formal presentations with accountants present also give workers an opportunity to point out where causal relationships depicted on the financial statements are in error. This opportunity to correct inaccurate cost assignments would be hard to match by any other means. It is timely and comes right from those who do the actual work.

Another approach is to post certain key financial numbers in each work area. They typically reflect the whole company, the local facility, and the work unit. Measures are a key element of TQM, and financial measures include return on assets employed, material consumed, indirect material, labor hours, maintenance costs, warranty costs, and other factors that workers' daily activities influence directly. In companies where quality indicators are posted, financial indicators can be posted too, not to inspire compromise between the two, but to illustrate that less variation in output leads to lower costs.

In many companies, key indicators are posted in each work unit. The total quality approach has led to defining a number of such indicators, displayed on a *five-up chart*. The indicators commonly used are:

1. Average defects per unit, where all the defects in a product line, from beginning to end, are added and divided by the number of units.
2. Outgoing quality audits.
3. Initial field quality.
4. Warranty claims.
5. Cost of poor quality.

The only one of these that uses financially expressed information is the last, the cost of poor quality. Recall that accounting will be assigned to calculate the cost of quality in most TQM implementations, so the framework for this indicator will already have been established.

The five-up chart can be expanded to include other information as well. Cost per unit, material per unit, indirect material, average time per machine changeover, internal services consumed, or production value per dollar of capital investment may be posted for each operating unit or shop. Enterprise-wide information such as operating margin, net income, backlog of orders, and even stock price may also be posted.

Which of these are best for any particular company will depend on the company and its circumstances. For example, some might feel that order backlog leads to too much distractive worry and insecurity when the backlog is reduced or eliminated, even though that could be an indicator of superior customer response times. Stock price is often thought to lead to concentration on the short-term, rather than on continuous improvement.

Each organization must reach its own conclusions as to what accounting information to provide to the whole workforce and how best to integrate that information into the total information picture that is revealed. Each will also have to decide whether to present its information in live briefings or by posting it, and how much explanation and feedback is best in its situation and culture. The important point is that since workers are asked to join the continuous improvement team for the good of the whole company, they deserve to know how their work unit is doing and how the whole company is doing in aggregate terms. They deserve financial information on a regular basis. Financial information, like other information, should be presented by the company itself, not read in the newspaper. By sharing information with our associates, we make it possible for them to adapt to changes in the company's overall situation and to contribute to improving it. We win our asso-ciates' confidence and make them a part of the company team.

INCENTIVE PAY PLANS

The purpose of total quality management is to provide more value for society by providing more value for the organization's customers. Increased value is accomplished through better quality, both in terms of the product's or ser-vice's ability to meet the customers' requirements and in terms of its freedom from defects. Better quality leads to happier customers, improved competi-tive position, and more profits to share among a firm's stakeholders.

One way to share these benefits with employees is through pay plans that scale rewards to results. Although the emphasis in a TQM implementation is more likely to be on sharing than on incentive, such plans are so widely called *incentive plans* that we will use that term here.

There are a number of philosophies that are employed in developing such plans. In some cases, the approach is "We all win or lose together." In these cases, a form of profit sharing, usually non-contributory, or a profit-based bonus will probably fit the need. Another way for employees to share in company-wide profits is through an Employee Stock Ownership Plan (ESOP). An ESOP has the added advantages of wedding the employee more firmly to the company and of helping focus on its long-term success.

In other cases, the whole company seems too remote, and its results are out of the control or visible influence of the individual worker. In these cases, profit-based incentives can be provided as for enterprise-wide plans, but they can be based on local results.

In still other cases, the incentives are brought right down to the individual worker's contributions. These cases include Nucor's famous pay plan for production above a base (which amounts to piecework, a highly unfashion-able but effective way of making each worker truly responsible for his own results, at least within the capabilities of the system he is given). More recently, pay plans that pay for skills give increasing rates to employees who learn and become certified in added work skills. The idea is that the ability to perform a number of jobs improves efficiency directly through added flexi-bility, as well as indirectly through mutual appreciation of one another's needs and improved cooperation. Such plans are especially helpful where self-directed work teams are used, because they allow the team more flexi-bility in planning and executing its work.

Each type of plan has pluses and minuses that make it desirable in some cases and less so in others. ESOPs, in particular, have legal and tax conse-quences that make them an often attractive approach for a company that is not closely held. They allow a tax benefit for issuing stock that is not available when selling stock to outsiders, but they do not require expenditure of cash that may be needed for growth.

All such pay plans have implications for the success of a TQM implementation, of course, but also have legal restrictions and implications. In addition, they require coordination with unions in unionized firms. Therefore, any plan adopted must be designed with the help of personnel experts, legal counsel, and any unions that represent the workers. An industrial psychologist among the personnel representatives might be valuable, and should be considered.

A cash pay-out plan that is especially suited to total quality management is *gainsharing*. Some plans that go under the name gainsharing today are really profit sharing, in that they pay a share of net income, or of net income above some base, to employees. This kind of plan does not depend on continuous improvement in that the base is constant. It may be a constant dollar amount or a formula based on some nominal return on equity or return on assets, but it rewards profit above the base even if it is not a gain, but a reduction from previous periods.

The term "gainsharing" as used here, however, means a plan for sharing the results of improvement, as measured by financial yardsticks. That is, it rewards employees when the company increases its profit. The profit may be measured as net income for the company in total or for individual plants or product lines.

In some companies, improvements in product or service cost are rewarded regardless of the net income. This is because the production and service workers can influence cost, but marketing, sales, and external market forces determine price received. Since net income is a result of both price and cost, it is felt that it is unfair to the workers to base their gainsharing on forces beyond their influence. Gainsharing based on cost improvement bases payouts only on costs that workers can affect.

In other companies improvements in net income are used as a base, because the price received for a product is influenced by its quality. In these cases, plan designers feel that workers can influence both parts of the net income computation. They also feel that "We are all in it together," so whatever happens, we share in the outcome.

Whichever basis of calculation is selected, and whatever the size of the unit over which gainsharing is to be calculated and distributed, the idea is that TQM is a customer focused continuous improvement approach. Improving quality benefits customers, and participation in the bottom-line results of that benefit is an aspect of participation that is worth considering.

An example of an incentive pay plan was developed at Borg-Warner Chemicals. Borg-Warner Chemicals produced ABS plastics and distributed them to manufacturers for making plastic parts and products, until the division was sold to General Electric following a leveraged buyout of the parent company, which required retirement of heavy debt load.

Using the balance sheet as a base, and applying the parent's cost of capital, a cost of capital could be charged to each center. In addition, a "management fee" for home office services was levied. The management fees appear to have been more or less arbitrary, since it was based on the contribution realized by each service center. As a result, more profitable service centers were allocated more management fees, whether they used more services from the home office or not. Using the Plastics Service Centers' conventional P&Ls, with capital charges and management fees deducted, yielded a contribution to total company profit. Twenty-five percent of this *residual contribution* (as the company called it) was distributed to the each service center as added compensation.

Although this scheme has a flaw in its allocation of management fees, since they bear no relation to services actually used, it is otherwise noteworthy in several ways:

1. It bases compensation on unit performance at the bottom line, not a subsidiary unit that could suboptimize profit center performance for local gain.
2. It considers possible trade-offs among capital, labor, freight, outside services, and material costs by measuring results at the bottom line, including a capital charge based on assets actually used.

As a final test, we can note that the first center using this system saw a 20 percent increase in revenues in the first year. The fun of running their own "small business" within the corporation was an added incentive to the managers and to others. It engendered a feeling of team participation and shared reward. This plan unfortunately went no further because General Electric didn't see it as fitting their corporate policies and canceled it after the buyout.

These plans illustrate a number of points:

1. Incentive pay plans work.
2. Incentive pay plans can be used to create participation and team spirit throughout an organization.
3. Incentive pay plans, at least within a TQM implementation, should not become a disguise for piecework. They should instead be built on a base of secure income for each participant.

4. Incentive pay plans work best when the incentives are based on performance of a unit small and local enough to be within the awareness of each participant, but large enough to avoid temptations to suboptimize.

In conclusion, incentive pay plans will almost certainly be considered some time in the development of a total quality initiative in any company. They should be considered for what they can do and for their limitations. Developing one that works will require participation by accounting, personnel, unions, and legal staffs, or by outsiders who can fill these roles.

INFORMATION THAT MANAGERS AND WORKERS WILL USE

At a number of points in our earlier discussions, we noted that operating managers usually are not satisfied with the accounting information they receive. The Institute of Management Accountants's *Management Accounting in the New Manufacturing Environment* reveals that 62 percent of the users of accounting information are not satisfied with what they get. Even 54 percent of those who prepare the information, the accountants themselves, feel it needs improvement.

More disturbing, cases are frequently cited where management says it likes its accounting system but has separate analyses made for actual decisions such as design trade-offs, production planning, make-or-buy, and capital investment. Such analyses are made by production analysts and engineers, rather than accountants, and even the accountants accept this as normal. The fact is that accounting information is often seen as irrelevant to actually running the business, and is ignored.

What can we do to make accounting information serve its real purpose? How can we meet our customers' requirements? Table 10-1 shows what respondents told the researchers at the IMA.

As you can see, some of these improvement areas overlap (like numbers 2 and 4) but they both refer to direct costing. Others are contradictory (like numbers 3 versus 5 or numbers 2 and 4 versus 6).

Since this survey is arranged in Pareto order, we can see where the emphasis should be placed. Number 1 refers to activity-based costing principles, number 2 to direct costing principles, and number 3 to elimination of standards as Dr. Deming suggests. All three of these are in keeping with the requirements of economic decision theory and all of the first four are in accordance with total quality requirements. The fact that contradictory suggestions appear confirms our earlier observation that each organization is different from every other, and has unique needs.

Table 10-1. Improvement Areas for Product Costing

Area of Improvement	% of Respondents
1 Develop alternative bases for assigning overhead costs to products	50
2 Minimize allocation of indirect cost	34
3 Shift toward actual costing	29
4 Shift toward variable costing	25
5 Shift toward standard costing	21
6 Shift toward full costing	18

To determine the needs of a particular company requires conducting investigations within the company itself. This means surveys, requests for criticism sent with reports, and mutual cross-representation on quality circles between accountants and users.

Although certain areas for improvement are likely to surface, as shown by the IMA research, we can't be sure which are foremost in any particular company until we look. For this reason, once a consultant is engaged, no specific changes should be proposed until the initial investigation is complete.

Another outcome of an initial review of a company's needs is that we will discover what decisions are most critical at the present moment. We can then concentrate first on reporting the information that will have the most impact. For example, changes in direct labor cost are important if added production is contemplated that will exceed present nominal capacity. But they are less important if direct labor workers are idle due to lack of work; for this decision direct labor workers are a fixed or sunk cost that is already committed and will not be changed. In the same way, supervision is a fixed cost if we consider adding capacity by enlarging an existing shop; it is a variable when deciding whether to add a shift. The point is that conventional cost accounting does not allow us to conveniently separate costs for such purposes.

To help separate costs in useful ways, Part 2 of this book has combined activity-based costing and direct costing techniques to work together. The methods we've developed allowed many existing cost systems to meet total quality requirements and users' criticisms as well. It may be necessary to redefine cost centers and allocation bases and to reformat some reports, but the basic mechanisms are already part of most automated cost systems.

By now, the application pattern should be clear:

1. Involve the customer.
2. Find out what the customer wants and needs.
3. Apply economic theory and accounting practices to provide such products.

To elaborate on these three points, recall that customer involvement is achieved through quality circle and action team membership. Finding out what the customer wants and needs is achieved through such market research methods as surveys and focus groups. These techniques will normally be used by action teams whose charters are to improve accounting information for operating departments. The action teams may be assisted or guided by the TQM office in applying these techniques. Finally, economic theory and accounting practices are employed through such techniques as standard costing, activity-based costing, and direct costing, as each company finds most useful in its circumstances.

Applying these principles leads to better decision support information. Data is available for special requirements like capital investment evaluation as well as for daily management of operations within both line and staff departments. It shows that the advantages of direct costing and activity-based costing are not mutually exclusive.

Finally, we have seen that certain performance information can be shared with workers in each functional area. Such information is especially helpful where self-directed work teams are used, since all the workers participate directly in management of their functions. Such summary performance information can be added to the posted charts that total quality companies often use to show quality data.

Summary information posted in work areas can include units or dollar value produced per dollar of capital investment (a more understandable version of the conventional measures *return on assets* or *internal rate of return*). It can also include such measures as labor hours or dollars per unit, material dollars per unit, dollars of scrap and rework, maintenance expenditures per unit of product, labor hours involved in setups and changeovers, and any other measures that are useful for quickly gauging a work unit's success in meeting its goals.

Sharing information encourages teamwork. It fosters intelligent allocation of improvement effort. Sharing financial information is often perceived as a real test of management's sincerity in its TQM implementation, since it is traditionally confined to management levels almost as if it were some kind of secret magic that only managers could understand and use.

Accounting information that is developed "in a corner," that addresses generalized needs of hypothetical, textbook firms, or that is kept from the workers whose actions give it shape will not be used. Accounting information that is developed with the cooperation of users, that meets the organization's immediate needs, and that is made available to those who can respond to it is information that will be used to carry on the business.

STATISTICAL CONTROL TECHNIQUES AND ACCOUNTING INFORMATION

Those who have followed the total quality movement for some time, who have read or heard Dr. Deming or Dr. Juran, or who have examined production-oriented TQM materials probably noticed the heavy emphasis on statistical quality control. On first examination it is difficult to see how accounting information can be used in a statistical control application, but a moment's reflection shows that accounting information is measurement data, just like physical measurements of manufactured products. The difference is that accounting information measures the operating characteristics of a business organization rather than the physical characteristics of an object.

Accounting information, therefore, is less immediate and harder to tie to individual actions. On the other hand, its aggregated nature allows conclusions about whole classes of activities that the individual actions make up. In the same way that successive measurements of the dimension of a drilled hole tell us when the drill is not operating properly, successive measurements of the organization through its accounting information can tell us when the economic entity is no longer operating as expected. Then we can look for special causes.

When accounting information indicates special causes of deviant performance, the cause may be internal, and the organization may no longer be operating as it was (differently from its previously determined process capability). If the new conditions are an improvement, we want to identify the special causes of change so we can continue to operate better. If they reveal degraded performance, we want to correct the special causes. If the special causes are outside the organization, such as a new entrant in the market or a national recession, we want to adapt to the new situation by altering the company's policies, marketing, or other factors to give the best results under the new external conditions.

The procedures for establishing statistical control over organizational behavior, as measured by accounting data, are the same as those for establishing statistical control over mechanical behavior as measured by physical data:

1. Establish the process capability.
2. Create a control chart.
3. Take periodic measurements and plot them on the chart.
4. Look for deviations or deviant patterns.
5. Investigate the causes of deviations.
6. Perpetuate good effects or correct the causes of bad ones.

A *control chart* uses measures of a process to determine the normal behavior of that process. In this case, we might look at something as simple as daily cash balances. We obtain regular measures of those balances and plot the mean as a line on a chart. The statistical measure *standard deviation* is a measure of variability that can also be calculated. Statisticians tell us that a standard normal distribution of the data predicts that about 95 percent of observations fall in two standard deviations of the mean and 99.7 percent fall in a band three standard deviations on either side of the mean. Drawing such bands on the chart, then plotting future data as events occur, tells us whether the new data is in accordance with the expected results. If it is not, we infer that something unusual may have happened and we can look for the cause. Such causes are called *special causes* to differentiate them from the *common causes* of variability that have always been present and that caused the variation included in the previous observations. Common causes are accounted for in the computation of mean and standard deviation that were used to construct the control chart.

Of course, processes are harder to define for an entire organization than for a shop or machine in a factory. Fortunately, we don't have to define "the process" quite as definitely as with a physical production process. We can call the process simply *organizational functioning, financial results of operations,* or some similar comprehensive name. Such sweeping and seemingly amorphous titles are workable because the organizational characteristics that interest accounting customers are already well defined. Of course, we will find new measures through applying total quality techniques to accounting information and processes, but we can begin with well-known measures that we already have. Table 10-2 shows some measures that are used for assessing overall organizational performance.

These characteristics are all measured and can be easily placed on statistical control charts. An advantage of applying statistical techniques to financial data is that we don't have to wait to get the measurements for establishing the process capability. It has already been collected as part of the

Table 10-2. Measures for Organizational Performance

Characteristic	Measure
Operating efficiency	Return on assets
Financial efficiency	Return on equity
Financial leverage	Debt/equity ratio
Short-term stability	Current ratio
Immediate stability	Quick ratio or "acid test"
Effectiveness	Market share and growth

historical accounting process. Stable firms in mature industries may be able to use these measures as "raw data" in making up their control charts.

Table 10-3 suggests some possible special causes of deviation that may arise in business and lists some possible special causes.

The possible causes shown in Table 10-3 are not all the possibilities, of course, but they illustrate the kinds of things that can happen to a business. We hope that our business intelligence is good enough that we get indications of these kinds of changes before they occur, but we may not. The real advantage of statistical analysis is that it tells whether variations in financial performance are significant or are within normal variability limits. We can tell because new data will fall outside the established control limits of the chart, or a deviant pattern will appear. Recall that deviant patterns include a series of points that, though each within the control limits, all tend in the same direction, or that all lie on the same side of the mean. So it doesn't take a wildly deviant point to indicate a new set of conditions within the firm or in the business environment. The ability to detect these more subtle shifts in performance is the advantage of statistical analysis of accounting data. Out-of-control results will be apparent anyway.

The examples of possible special causes of deviant financial measures in Table 10-3 indicate one that is recurring and expected—seasonality. Some businesses produce results that vary from season-to-season in a regular, predictable pattern. There may be other patterns as well, but the most common

Table 10-3. Causes of Deviation

Characteristic	Measure	Possible Causes
Operating efficiency	Return on assets	Price changes Resource scarcity New plant or equipment
Financial efficiency	Return on equity	Operating changes as above Stock/debt swap Extraordinary gains or losses (as selling a division or subsidiary)
Financial leverage	Debt/equity ratio	Stock/debt swap Large gains or losses Stock issue or buyback
Short-term stability	Current ratio	Seasonal purchasing patterns Adverse trend
Immediate stability	Quick ratio or "acid test"	Same as for current ratio
Effectiveness	Market share and growth	New competitors New products or technology Change in customer tastes or industries

is seasonality. Each business's executives are acquainted with the recurring cycles of their industry and their company. If the financial measures that are charted can be adjusted for known, expected changes such as seasonality, the statistical dispersion will be much smaller and special causes of deviation will be evident sooner or at lower levels.

The procedure for calculating seasonality factors is the same one used by the Department of Commerce for calculating *seasonally adjusted* national economic activity indices. It requires more data points than simple mean and standard deviation calculations, but an advantage of accounting data is that we usually have enough history to allow such calculations at low cost.

Statisticians who may be reading this immediately recognize the mathematical procedure. For others, note that it involves setting up a distinct variable for each season (or actually all but one, which serves as the "base" for the seasonal variation). When data represents spring, the "spring" variable is assigned a coefficient of one and the others are zero. In the same way, each season's variable is given a coefficient of one when the data represents that season. A regression analysis is run on the resulting expressions and tests of significance are made to determine whether the seasonality factors are worth using to evaluate future data.

If all this is too hard to figure out, don't worry. You'll want a statistician to work it out for you anyway. The point is that adjustments can be made for recurring seasonal variation. The same technique can be used to account for any variable that changes regularly and predictably, allowing business data to be charted after it has been "normalized." For example, an adjustment may be desirable to allow for a known trend that increases or decreases costs or sales. This will remove one cause of variation. With a known cause removed, variation will be smaller and variation due to other causes will be more readily apparent. Special cause investigations can be directed only to cases where special causes are likely to be present.

So far, the examples cited have involved the business as a whole. Control charting can be applied to accounting data at department and other levels as well. Personnel counts, hours, material costs, indirect material costs, utilities, and maintenance are all candidates for control charting.

A further advantage of control charts for accounting data is that it makes the presentation of such data much more understandable. Managers who are visually oriented can understand the message at a glance and can use the information more readily.

Total quality accounting fits into the total quality management picture in a number of ways, including the use of statistical control charts. A difference is that, because the function of accounting is to produce information on the business as a whole, accounting data can be used to detect special causes in overall business processes. It can also be used to detect special causes of variation that may occur within organizational components. A refinement is that seasonality or other adjustments can be used to remove predictable effects so that special causes can be found more readily.

CAPITAL ALLOCATION—A TOTAL QUALITY COLLABORATIVE PROCESS*

Capital asset acquisition is becoming increasingly important as industrial organizations turn from old-style functional production departments to product-oriented work flows. Both new technology and total quality management demand continued capital expenditures. Even after new financial models are developed, they cannot be allowed to become the sole factor determining capital allocation. All aspects of corporate performance must contribute to the capital allocation process so that future capabilities and capacities are aligned with requirements of the new competitive environment.

Here is a process of capital allocation that allows capital projects to compete in an open forum where all aspects of the decision can be considered. They compete among all alternatives, receiving thorough review at the strategic level as well as at the financial and local plant levels.

In the organization where this effort began, capital asset planning had been done in a cell of about 12 people whose work consisted solely of equipment planning and purchasing. Over many years they had partially insulated themselves from the production engineering and production departments and had completely insulated themselves from the quality assurance and financial departments. This method had the benefit of allowing experimentation that might not have passed financial scrutiny, but it unfortunately also resulted in some purchases that didn't fit with the desired strategic direction. In addition, there was an emphasis on committing the entire capital allocation each year, so long-term developments were sometimes neglected in favor of easy purchases near year-end. As part of a total quality management implementation the company began to address these deficiencies. They realized that any capital asset acquisition program must consider three factors:

1. Strategic plans.
2. Economic returns.
3. Current production requirements.

---

*This section is adapted from an article by the author, published in the *Production and Inventory Management Journal, 3rd quarter, 1992.*

To address all three factors while adopting total quality management required them to open the process to all elements of the organization that could contribute.

Total Quality Management is Participative

After deciding that participation from many disciplines was needed to ensure rational, effective capital allocation in a total quality environment the question was: which disciplines? The following answers emerged:

1. *Production engineering*—To provide for today's production needs requires knowing what today's workload is and what the present capabilities are. Workload planning and production engineering have that information. Therefore, personnel from workload planning and production engineering became part of the capital allocation process.

2. *Marketing*—To provide for future production needs, we must know what those needs will be. Marketing can project future workload types and volumes. It can forecast capacity requirements. Therefore, marketing became part of the capital allocation process.

3. *Production departments*—Someone must actually operate the equipment, turning its capability into usable products. Therefore, the equipment must be operable and maintainable; it must serve the needs of its users. Production personnel will actually use the items purchased, so they can best evaluate an item's utility within existing processes. Production became part of the capital allocation process.

4. *Finance*—When equipment is bought, it must serve production needs efficiently. Mere convenience is not enough; it must reduce costs below those of alternatives. But interested parties are likely to bias their analyses. Financial and accounting personnel can provide an unbiased review of costs. In addition, the controller is charged with monitoring expenditure of funds and with cost reporting. These responsibilities include capital expenditures and costs incurred in the use of capital equipment. Therefore, financial personnel became part of the capital allocation process.

5. *Headquarters*—Where capital is allocated for sites or divisions to spend without overall review of individual projects, less favorable projects at some sites may supersede better ones at different sites. Consequently, headquarters became involved to ensure uniform analysis for comparison purposes, to provide a "big picture" strategic focus, and to act as arbitrator among divisions as each advocated its own preferences.

Benchmarking and Best Practices are TQM Tools

Having determined who could best contribute to the capital allocation process, the next question was what mechanism should be used. Two models were found that contributed to the capital allocation process. The companies using them are different and use them for different reasons, but aspects of both were employed.

1. *The ITT example*—ITT under Harold Geneen began years ago to operate the company as a matrix, with operating and financial lines reporting to headquarters separately. The company did not want to adopt that model in total because it did not fit its production-oriented culture and because vertical staff liaison without full participation at the local level was part of the original problem. But one implication proved effective in allocating scarce capital to the best available projects. In that model, subsidiary, division, and plant management met annually in a large, amphitheater-like room. Each division presented a performance review for the last year. They were subjected to questioning and criticism by other divisions and headquarters staff. Part of these presentations was a discussion of capital investment plans for the coming year. Because of the potentially hostile atmosphere, each project had to be thoroughly examined and analyzed. Any flaws in the analysis were likely to be discovered. Although unanimity is impossible in such a large, competitive group, a decision could be reached on which projects to accept. The financing came from headquarters, where capital is managed.

2. *The 3M example*—3M uses a slightly different system for allocating capital to new projects. The system is different because 3M is more innovative and creates new divisions for new product lines. Consequently, peer approval is less important. In 3M's case, each manager who wants capital allocated for a new product line or for expansion makes a presentation to a review board. The board consists of members of the headquarters staff and a number of managers of divisions that have successfully grown from start-up status. Thus, company-wide strategies, economic considerations, and operating experience are all represented on the board. The board allocates capital. Its bias is to fully fund a project or turn it down. Partial funding is almost never considered because a few successful projects are preferred to many that never quite get going.

Reviewing these two examples yielded three common factors to incorporate in the capital allocation process:

1. Presentation of competing projects. This imposes discipline on the operating managers and equipment planners to do thorough analysis.

2. Projects compete within the whole capital pool. There are no subsidiary allocations and therefore reduced opportunity for suboptimal
   decisions by local managers.
3. Use of a board. In one case the board includes representatives of
   competing divisions, in the other it includes some members with
   similar backgrounds, but who do not represent competition for
   funds.

The Capital Allocation Method that Resulted

Once these principles were developed, actual functioning had to be defined
so that attention could be focused on projects whose cost justified the effort
of extensive review. Small items were excluded from the process by granting
local authority without review for purchase of assets below a dollar threshold. A decision was also made to grant authority for limited purchasing
above the threshold as an encouragement to innovation, but only up to a prescribed dollar total for each site.

In planning the bulk of future production capability and capacity, a larger
strategic view was needed. A big-picture view can achieve more rational and
productive allocation of capital spending authority to specific projects when
all projects compete without regard to which site originated them. As
described earlier, a corporate-level board seemed to be the best way to
achieve the necessary review. Making a live presentation also imposes discipline on the preliminary process used at the operating locations. Finally, a
live presentation to the capital allocation board ensures that each site gets its
"day in court."

The board consists of representatives from headquarters as well as from
the separate sites. An effort is made to ensure that the representatives are
chosen to include knowledge of the areas mentioned earlier: strategic
planning, workload planning, production engineering, production, and
finance. By including representatives of different sites and disciplines on
the board, decisions can be made without regard to which divisions might
"win" and which might "lose." Effectiveness and efficiency are the goals,
not equality.

Board members may not be presenters. Although each member from a
field location will naturally feel a need to advocate his own projects, he is
able to do so with less passion if he is not also a presenter. Presenters may
have staff assistance to answer questions from the board. Presenters enter the
board meeting to make their pitch and then leave. They do not attend one
another's presentations. After hearing the site representatives present their
projects, the capital allocation board decides which projects to recommend to

the chief executive. In their deliberations members may recall presenters or staff members to ask specific questions.

The capital allocation board's final function is to receive post-installation reviews of projects approved in the preceding two or three years. These reviews are performed by a review team that reports to the board.

Difficulties with the New Method

This method of capital allocation can excite resistance from some locations. When resistance is encountered, it arises from two sources: the natural tendency to want control of one's own affairs, without "outside interference," and fear by those now doing capital allocation that any deficiencies can no longer be hidden.

The first, the desire of organizations to resist giving up control of their affairs, is understandable but must be overcome for the best overall results.

The second, the apprehension of those who now do capital equipment planning, may be well founded. In at least one plant, outside consultants and some internal departments repeatedly demonstrated that they planned without considering important operational segments or strategic direction. In at least that one case some discipline and rigor were overdue.

A more substantial difficulty is that this procedure added a step to the acquisition process.

Advantages of the New Method

When all capital spending authority is pooled (after allocation of local authority for smaller items), projects can be selected for their contribution to company-wide needs rather than to local survival needs, so that suboptimal choices are reduced.

Another major plus is that formal presentation of each project imposes discipline on local planners. To make a winning presentation they are forced to include all affected parties in the local planning process. A winning analysis must be rigorous and complete. Added impetus to a disciplined approach arises from the post-installation review because poor estimates of need, utilization, and benefit will be exposed.

Together, these three factors produce rational allocation of capital to productive ends. There are fewer replacements of like equipment where newer technologies would be better. There are fewer "white elephants." Capital equipment purchases support strategic plans, rather than having to make strategic plans around existing capabilities.

Conclusion

Fragmented methods of capital allocation often do not take account of strategic or business plans, they can allow sloppy analysis, and they can be unresponsive to organizational changes that result from adopting new production methods.

Using a board that includes operating site participation and that represents all affected functional areas ensures support of the strategic plan, imposes discipline on the local analysis process, and can improve efficiency in purchasing.

This method of capital allocation allows all affected parties to participate in accordance with total quality management principles.

The New Capital Allocation Process in Action—Participative Acquisition Made a Difference

In the three years before we began participative capital budgeting, microcomputers were purchased by production and engineering managers whenever they could free some money.

In my own case, I asked for a microcomputer and heard nothing for some weeks. Then one morning I found a stack of boxes on my office floor. I had to unpack, assemble, and connect what was then new and unfamiliar equipment. The assembly job was harder because parts were missing; it took some experimentation to find out what I still needed.

When I investigated I found out that my experience was typical. There were microcomputers from Tandy, Zenith, IBM, and a number of others; many were not compatible and were usable only by those who had ordered them. There were also two or three (the lack of standardization and control made the exact numbers uncertain) small LANs in various buildings around the facility.

To avoid future problems of this kind, total quality management principles led to forming a team composed of three equipment specialists, three software specialists, and representatives of the engineering, production, finance, and material departments.

To prepare a recommendation for corporate review, a meeting was arranged with representatives of other facilities where a standard package was selected. Secondary software was also chosen for applications where the integrated package might not be adequate.

After the required presentation and approval steps, the team devised an installation process wherein each machine was completely unpacked and set up. It was run in, software was installed, and it was tested. It was then repackaged and delivered by an equipment specialist and a software specialist working together. The user received basic instruction and a contact number for additional assistance. Finally, follow-up instruction was provided after a week to ten days.

More than six hundred microcomputers were installed this way in eight months. Each user received a machine that was up and running in his own work space with software installed, including a few help screens the installation team devised themselves. No one repeated my experience trying to make it work, since all had instruction provided with the machine. After installation, workers had the added benefit of sharing both data and operating techniques. Once they solved a problem, it was solved for everyone, and when a LAN was later installed, there were no compatibility problems. As an added benefit, adding a $60 emulation board to many of them allowed us to replace mainframe terminals that had cost nearly $3000 a year for maintenance alone.

11

PUTTING IMPROVED ACCOUNTING PROCEDURES TO WORK

Our discussion of total quality accounting began with part 1 discussing total quality in general, and how certain precepts and practices can be used to do things better. Part 2 then discussed some of the ways accounting has developed and is changing to meet total quality requirements. Here in part 3, the last few chapters repeated that pattern, focusing more tightly on total quality precepts applied to accounting functions. We examined participation with the accounting department's customers and suppliers then discussed a few ways of improving accounting products. These "new, improved" accounting products can enhance organizational performance through their contribution to better management in all functional areas of the company.

These kinds of improvements are more important than improvements in the accounting department's internal processes. For the accounting department, product improvements are more important than process efficiency because accounting reports on the whole organization, so that any product improvement there is likely to improve operations everywhere. The accounting function itself consumes only a small portion of an organization's resources, so there is a much smaller base upon which process improvements within that function can work. In addition, improved accounting products benefit the accounting process in the same way they benefit any other process, through providing information for better management.

Nevertheless, there are two important reasons to improve the internal accounting processes of a company:

1. Even if they consume a small part of the company's total resources, that part is the part accounting management is responsible for, and it should be used as effectively as possible.

2. As a department within a total quality company, the accounting department must undertake process improvements along with the rest of the company to remain a credible part of the overall management team.

In other words, better accounting is like any other improved product—it is more certain, cheaper, and faster. In a physical product, these improvements would be labeled "quality, cost, and delivery." Since they are the same as for any other product, a person might guess they can be achieved in the same ways. Such a guess would be right.

Now that we have reviewed some ways to make improved accounting products and seen some examples of improved products, the question remains, "How can we improve our internal processes? How can we not only do better accounting, but how can we do accounting better?" In this respect, accounting is no different from any other process in an organization. It can be done better by designing and using processes that reduce variability, so the outputs mean the same thing every time they are produced. It can also be done better by doing it cheaper, conserving resources. Finally, it can be done better by doing things faster, producing information nearer the time of the underlying activities reported on. This is accounting's equivalent of time-based competition.

So to begin at the beginning, with the first area of improvement, how can we ensure our products exhibit minimum variability, that they mean the same thing every time they are produced?

Here are four techniques that can reduce the variability of accounting reports. They also apply to any process, but we will examine them here in an accounting process context:

1. Freeze configuration.
2. Release modifications in blocks.
3. Use statistical quality control.
4. Establish error-checking routines.

Freeze configuration means that once information, such as a report or chart, is approved and placed into regular distribution, it should not be changed. Users will appear with many suggestions for improvement when they get new information, but those should be picked up in the design and validation stages. Once the information begins to be circulated, any changes in format, content, or arithmetic will mean that one period's report is not comparable to another's. The usefulness of the information is thereby reduced.

More importantly for the current discussion of process variability, changing the information keeps the preparer from learning a regular routine; the process is not allowed to stabilize. With no stable process, there can be no determination of process capability and therefore no statistical control. Put another way, when every time is a change, there are no reliable rules, and there can be no assurance of the product's "goodness" or even of its definition. Thus, it can not be used with assurance by managers or workers and its value is limited.

Release modifications in blocks means that we can accumulate improvement recommendations. Then, from time to time, we can change the product and the process as needed. Incorporating all changes at each change date allows a new product definition and a new process, with a new process capability. All users can learn the new product, the workers can learn the new process, and we can once again have a stable system. Recalling that a stable system, one in mathematical statistical control, is a requirement for total quality improvement efforts, we see that only by limiting product and process changes can we have improvable processes.

. Another advantage of block modifications is a reduction in operating cost that flows from stable processes. Quality assurance checks can be limited when the process is stable and trustworthy. Requirements to learn new procedures, with attendant error rates and inefficiencies, are reduced. Block modifications thereby improve both the accounting product and the operating efficiency of the accounting department.

The third method of improving accounting quality is to use *statistical process control*. Statistical process control shows what our process capability is, so we know what we are trying to improve. It also shows when deviations from that capability have occurred, so causes can be sought and corrected. Finally, statistical control of accounting processes brings the accounting department into the TQM process in a way that is understandable to the production workers who must use accounting information and who therefore must have confidence in its reliability.

While we often think that accountants make few errors, we still need to answer Deming's question, "How do you know?" When one company looked for an answer, it found that the production functions aimed for 200 parts per million as a reject rate, and were approaching that goal, but accounting functions made 6,000 errors per million actions. Surely if they can do it, we can, and we must to preserve our credibility. So an answer to the question, "How do you know?" is "With statistical process control."

Charts can be made for each job, if desired, and posted where the responsible worker can see them. Whether to make them visible to others is a matter of local choice, depending on the level of teamwork and trust in the work section. In general it is probably better not to post them openly, since it can make the worker feel threatened rather than feeling inspired to improve the process. Remember the TQM principle that problems are seldom in the worker; they are almost certainly in the process, tools, or training.

One company has used a number of techniques and devised what it calls its daily management system. Each worker has defined a most important job. That job is flow charted and indicators of quality and efficiency are developed and charted. These indicators are chosen based on seven factors:

1. Quantifiable and measurable.
2. Customer focused.
3. Supportive of objectives.
4. Repeatable.
5. Simple.
6. Acceptable.
7. Sensitive to variability.

These criteria allow selection of characteristics that are charted and examined for improvement opportunities. Some that were selected are:

1. Data errors (prices, rates, counts, etc.).
2. Arithmetic errors.
3. Time from date of request (disbursement voucher, expense report, or other source document from outside) to date of response (check, report, transaction research reply, or other response).
4. Requests from customers for clarification or follow-up information (an indicator of information inadequacy to the customers' purposes).

Besides control charts for characteristics of each worker's most important job, charts can be made for each process, regardless of the number of workers involved. Such control charts can be used together with flow charts of the process to find improvement opportunities. They may be posted for all to see as a way of helping generate suggestions for improvement "from the floor." They can also be used by quality circles and action teams in their work.

The final suggestion for improved accounting processes is to establish *error-checking routines*. We have all seen spreadsheet auditor programs. The same principles of checking totals across and down, doing arithmetic in several ways, and comparing results can be applied to any process involving numeric conclusions.

There are two basic ways of error checking:

1. Perform the process twice in parallel, and compare the results.
2. Create a feedback loop, where the final result is compared to the beginning data to see that the conclusions correspond to related data, or even that they are simply "reasonable in the circumstances."

The first method, *performing the process in parallel*, is wasteful, since each action must be done in duplicate. Also, if one turn through a process is erroneous, the second may be as well. Hard-to-read data can be misread the same way twice and the error repeated in the parallel processes. It should only be used where no other check is possible and where the risk of error is high enough to warrant the cost. It was once used in data entry through punch cards, and is still used for some data entry operations, but in general it is better to use feedback loops where possible.

The second method, *feedback loops*, involves checking results against source data to see that they fit. A feedback loop exists in inventory records, where rather than rechecking all transaction documents, their entry, and arithmetic, we simply go out and count the stuff to see whether it corresponds to the accounting results.

Under the same caption of error checking we can also consider error prevention through process design. Robust processes can produce good results even when minor breakdowns occur. Parallel processing and feedback loops are ways of making a process more robust. Another important feature of well-designed procedures is that it is easier and more natural to do them correctly than to do them wrong.

Ways of ensuring that correct entries are made include data-checking routines that reject charges where invalid job numbers are entered, or where production workers cannot draw material unless they are clocked into a job for which the desired items are on the bill of material. Integrated computer systems make such checking simple and natural once the programs are written and in place.

A purely accounting application of such an error-checking routine would require a valid vendor code before any disbursement check could be written. It would further check the invoice number to ensure that that invoice number was not already entered or paid for that vendor. Such routines are common practice in all commercially sold accounting programs today. They should also be an integral part of any custom programs written by your company.

These four techniques are well known but observed only where discipline is exercised to ensure they are followed. Although they have always been good practice in accounting systems design, they are especially valuable in total quality accounting processes to ensure total quality accounting products.

RE-ENGINEERING THE ACCOUNTING FUNCTION

In law school, every student learns the importance of precedent. In an oft-quoted passage, a trial judge says, ". . . the books are now too many to be overthrown. But if it had been a new case, it would have been interesting." In the same way, we too often treat the accounting books as "now too many to be overthrown." Both product and customer organizational patterns are familiar ways of looking at accounting functions, and our first response to a call for improvement is usually to look at these patterns for possibilities. Re-engineering, on the other hand, takes the accounting processes as "a new case." Re-engineering doesn't accept old, familiar patterns just because they are known. It treats the gathering and processing of accounting data into products as though it had not been done before. It starts with a clean slate.

Today's accounting departments are most often organized according to products, with sections for supplier disbursements, payroll disbursements, billing, analysis, and general ledger, among others. In these cases, transactions usually pass through several hands before completion. For example, an incoming supplier invoice may be routed to one person to be matched to purchase orders, another for receiving information, another to check the previous two, a fourth to enter the information into the check writing system, and a fifth to look at all of it again when the check is written.

Another organizational pattern is according to customer, as when plant controllers or project accountants are assigned to serve a single operating entity within a company. These customer-oriented accountants are dedicated to their customers. They process transactions for that customer from beginning to end. When a project manager wants accounting information, there is only one place to go. The same person or a small unit does all processing for that customer, including invoicing, disbursements (or disbursement voucher preparation for a central check-writing facility), and analysis. In this pattern, general ledger and payroll are usually separate services performed by outside groups, or even by external contractors.

These patterns may be best for a company, but re-engineering doesn't simply assume they will be. It uses the clean slate, with a total quality approach, to develop the accounting processes that are best for each organization. In re-engineering the accounting function, we expect a total quality effort to use the total quality principles of being customer focused, participatory, and data driven. And so it does.

To begin a total quality re-engineering effort, we begin with the principle of customer focus. Customer surveys, focus groups, and the issues raised in quality circles give information that can be used to define the accounting products not as they are, but as they ought to be. These tools allow us to define the products that customers really value. They also can be used to validate new product designs when completed.

The first step in re-engineering the accounting function, then, is to define the products that are to be produced. These should be defined as precisely as possible. At the same time, continuous improvement means that their redefinition will never be completed. As in everything, the re-engineering team must use judgment as to when the balance between precise definition of products and the need for action compels them to go forward to the next step.

The products that will be defined consist of recurring reports, tax filings, disbursements (checks or electronic transfers), invoices, and special analyses for upper management and operating managers and their staffs. They may also include live presentations. These products, like any product, consist of parts. The parts of accounting products are the data elements that are transformed by accounting processes into accounting products.

So the second step in re-engineering the accounting function is to see what component parts are used in making the accounting products. If they exist, flow charts of processes can be used to trace products back to their constituent elements. If they do not exist, but computer program documentation does, it can also be a way of getting back to the data elements that make up accounting products.

The third step will be largely done in accomplishing the first two, and might even be done before or concurrently with step two. It is to document the processes that turn the raw material of data elements into the information (such as reports or analyses) or physical products (such as disbursements or invoices) that go to our customers.

Defining these processes too broadly can lead us to revert to the traditional patterns. If accounting production processes are defined as "make disbursements" or "generate tax returns" they will naturally lead back to the traditional product-oriented pattern. If they are defined too narrowly as "calculate C from A and B" or "arrange data on report form" they will lead naturally to a work-process oriented pattern, where no one sees the whole product as it is worked on. Instead, both definitions of processes should be used. Again, a flow chart of the production process for each product is helpful. Such flow charts should be constructed, at least initially, without indicating who or what work unit actually does the work at present. The object, after all, is to determine what should be done and what work units ought to be created to do it, not what is now done or who does it in the current systems.

In constructing charts of accounting production processes, there will be times when the same data goes into more than one product, and when the output of an intermediate process feeds more than one product. For example, disbursement data feeds both P&L reporting and cash management. Payroll data feeds tax filings, product costing, departmental management reports, and payroll disbursements. These situations are illustrative of the choices that must be made: do we structure our work so that each worker does one kind of thing, so each worker does everything on one product, or so each worker does a variety of intermediate processes on various products? Should we use self-directed work teams that produce their products from beginning to end? What would such a concept do to internal control?

Each situation is unique, and there is no one answer. It can be observed that traditional patterns had each worker doing one kind of thing on one kind of product. These patterns are still prevalent, and consequently the success stories of cases where individuals or teams are responsible for products from beginning to end or for meeting all of a customer's accounting needs get considerable attention. Some such success stories include the insurance company that cut underwriting processing time from two weeks to seventeen minutes after learning that almost all the time was spent by documents moving, waiting, or being read by new processors. In that case, individuals were made responsible for each insurance policy's entire processing. Another success story involves work teams, where an accounting department was not restructured, but each existing section was made a self-directed work team. Cross-training occurred within teams, and much less directive management was needed. The team was responsible for choosing its own associates, and for its own products. Even in a growing company, staffing was gradually reduced by the teams themselves, and occasional consensual transfers among teams kept a "them and us" attitude from taking over.

As with many of the other practices used in TQM, the methods of developing processes, organizational patterns, and selecting tools have been borrowed from other management approaches. Here as elsewhere, TQM uses what works to achieve constant improvement.

One such method is used by computer programmers in "structured programming." This technique does not have a formal name that is in regular use, but it may have local names in different organizations. It is a simple visual technique of making a matrix with columns labeled as products, such as supplier checks, departmental management reports, special analyses, or general ledger entries. It is even more effective if the columns are specific reports, rather than a catch-all caption "departmental management reports." Rows may be either data elements or sources of data, depending on the purpose of the matrix at the moment. It is probably helpful to do it both ways to get different perspectives (see Figure 11-1).

Figure 11-1. Process Assessment Grid for Re-engineering an Accounting Function.

	Process Assessment Grid for Re-engineering and Accounting Function							
Report, Product or Output / **Data Source**	Department performance	Plant performance	Job/project cost	Disbursement	Paycheck	Inventory	Cash forecast	Financial statements
Labor Transactions	X	X	X		X		X	X
Material issues	X	X	X			X		X
Tool issues	X	X	X					
Invoices				X		X	X	X
Purchase orders				X			X	
Receiving reports				X		X		X

Intersections of rows and columns are marked with an X or darkened where a data element or a source of data feeds an output. Then, by trying different ways of ordering the rows and columns, it is possible to observe patterns and groupings of Xs or shading that indicate possible task groupings. Depending on the work volume, these tasks may be assigned to sections, teams, or individuals. They will be related through using the same data to produce similar products, and will thereby contribute to efficiency.

Of course, such patterns of Xs or shading are no magic solution to re-engineering an accounting function. They are merely one way of looking at the job and can be quite helpful. Other considerations are internal control, company culture, and the desire to centralize or to decentralize functions. Even looking at the example shows that other groupings of work are possible, such as according to input source.

To summarize our discussion of re-engineering accounting, we have seen that there are four steps:

1. Define the products.
2. Define the necessary data inputs.
3. Describe the processes that will be used to transform the inputs into products.
4. Determine who should do the processing.

There are established tools that can be helpful, such as flow charts and matrices, but the final recommendations must be the responsibility of the task force or action team that is responsible for the re-engineering effort.

As in any TQM initiative, such a group should include experts from an organization's accounting department as well as representatives of those who use the products and who supply the inputs. When a preliminary design is done, it can be validated by a separate board or committee.

One final thought on re-engineering the accounting function is that recent research (the Hackett study) has shown that the lowest-cost accounting pattern is to perform transaction processing centrally, preparing customer invoices, supplier payments, and standard reports at a central service center. Local analysis such as capital equipment requirements and special reports is best done at each site.

LIFE-CYCLE VALUE

Life-cycle value is a an advanced development of life-cycle costing. In *life-cycle costing* the cost of a proposed product is estimated for its whole life, including costs that conventional accounting methods would expense each period and would not assign to the product. Life-cycle value adds an analysis of the customer's perception of value provided by each cost element. It is then possible to determine which features are worth the cost to the customer and to provide a service or product that the customer will be glad to purchase.

To simplify our discussion, we will break down life-cycle value into two components, life-cycle cost and process value analysis. Combining these two aspects yields life-cycle value. Since life-cycle cost is more widely known and practiced, we will consider it first, then extend it into the more comprehensive concept of life-cycle value.

The practice of life-cycle costing is not unique to total quality accounting, but is one of the useful concepts adopted by total quality accountants in their quest to measure the total effect of each product on the firm.

Life-cycle cost is like cost of quality in that it takes information that is not aggregated in conventional financial statements and puts it in one analysis for management decisions. It includes research and development, which is expensed each period in conventional accounting, as a cost of the product. It includes design costs. It includes tooling and production planning. It includes shutdown costs at the end of the product life. And of course it includes the conventional costs of production. It may help to think of life-cycle costing as treating a product as if it were being set up as a free-standing, separate business.

You can see that this is a far more comprehensive cost statement than is typically prepared. Estimating these costs for a new product requires a TQM approach, with involvement by any affected parties, as shown in Table 11-1.

This looks a lot like an action team, and a crossfunctional action team is a good, "TQM" way to develop life-cycle costs for a new product. Where products are developed by product teams, as with the Dodge Viper and most new aircraft projects, life-cycle costing is part of the development team's job. It is one of the primary reasons that accountants are included as members of product development teams.

Table 11-1. Life-cycle costing

Functional Department	Contribution
Marketing	Performance and Features, Sales
Engineering	Design, Bill of Materials
Purchasing	Material Costs
Production Engineering	Tooling and Equipment, Processes
Production	Conversion Costs
Customer Service	Installation and Warranty
Finance	Cost of Capital

Progressing from life-cycle costing to life-cycle value requires adding process value analysis. Recall that process value analysis (PVA) seeks to find the value set by the customer for each feature of a product. It then compares that value to the cost of providing that feature, and eliminates steps that add cost, but not value.

In life-cycle value analysis, the marketing function is much more involved, because they don't just describe a desired product with its performance characteristics and features. Marketing must also set values on each level of achievable performance and on each feature. It must price these characteristics, to see how much revenue each will add to the total revenue stream expected from the product in its alternative configurations.

When prospective revenue streams have been defined for various possible product configurations, the values set by customers are known by the prices they will pay. Added or reduced revenues can be compared to added or saved costs to see which characteristics are worthwhile for the customer. In this way, a product is developed that will provide the best value-to-cost ratio for the customers who buy it.

Theoretical purists among us may have noticed that features are valued differently by different customers. While customer A may be willing to pay $1 for an added feature, that same feature may be worth $2 to customer B. In our discussion of cost-profit-volume analysis in part 2, we noted that some companies "segment the market" so they can charge these customers different prices and extract this value for themselves by charging different customers different prices. The example of airline tickets was presented, where fare restrictions and capacity management attempt to set a different price for each traveler. The amount customers would pay if they had to, but did not, is called "consumer surplus" in economic theory. Purists may also notice that if the consumer surplus is added to the price, and ranked on a graph from highest to lowest, the result is the product demand curve. Seeing it in these terms can assist marketing in their price-setting process. In large companies, such analysis may even be explicitly done by economists and market researchers.

Examining the possibilities of segmenting the market, even if it isn't practical to do so, aids in deciding whether to offer various models of a product, so as to give each customer what he most values. These complexities are another reason why a team approach, including everyone from marketing to production to accounting, is needed for top-quality decisions in this area.

It is clear that this is a repetitive process, where each combination of characteristics interacts in unique ways, so marketing can't simply make up a list of alternative product configurations and selling prices, then "throw them over the wall" to engineering. Engineering can't just "throw the design over the wall" to production engineering and purchasing. Rather, a team approach is essential to ensure that each department interacts with the others to arrive at an optimal product for the benefit of the company's customers.

We are skirting the edges of economic theory here, and it is worth a brief examination. If our firm provides services and products that a customer will gladly buy at the offering price, we have provided that customer with an improvement in his condition, evidenced by his willingness to buy from us. If we realize a higher profit, it is evidence that we have added more value than we consumed. In other words, by using life-cycle value analysis, we have maximized the total well-being of the world, by making the most valuable products while consuming the fewest resources. To accomplish the economic marvel of contributing to the betterment of the world while improving our own position, we must know the total cost and benefit of our new-product effort. This is accomplished through life-cycle value analysis.

12

GUERRILLA TQM

DOES YOUR COMPANY HAVE WHAT IT TAKES?

If total quality management only appears like a "flavor of the month" fix for your company, I can guarantee that it will never be completely accepted and practiced. In order for a total quality effort to succeed, it must lose its identity as a special effort. Complete acceptance by the organization will eventually lead TQM principles and practices to become the only way of doing business that the organization knows. It will no longer appear to be a distinct program, but will be just the way things are done in X Company.

Such a thorough incorporation of TQM into a company's style requires a number of factors working in its favor:

1. TQM requires commitment from the top; the chief executive must lead it, relentlessly and clearly.
2. Everything done must be related to how it serves internal or ultimate customers; TQM is customer focused.
3. A few goals must be established to guide the effort, goals everyone can see and recognize.
4. Results count; TQM is data driven; workers need data on present conditions to guide improvements and they need data on results to assess outcomes and guide further improvements.
5. TQM must be adapted to the organization; someone else's approach will work only if it is adapted to each organization's needs and situation.

We have covered these points in detail as we went along, but if one is lacking, can TQM still work? What if the chief executive won't provide committed leadership? What if he won't give it more than lip service, or declines to use TQM? Can it work if only a segment of the organization wants to use it?

The answer is that it can, but successes must inspire the CEO to move out front and take charge, or it will die out over time.

In a large industrial company, a small group of individuals in one facility wanted to be part of a total quality company. They wanted their employer to experience the benefits and revolutionary changes of TQM for the benefit of themselves, their fellow workers, and their customers. But they were unable to sell the corporate chief executive on a company-wide program. They could not get the necessary commitment of training resources. The CEO would not accept the risks of raising expectations or of altering established ways of managing. (Change is always scary, and risky too, so reluctance is understandable.) Further, while TQM will improve an organization's work in many ways, it won't solve all the problems; it isn't a magic cure-all.

Should a large company take such a risk? These people thought so. They saw that in some industries, those who were late to adopt total quality precepts are still catching up. Some have lost their competitive positions, apparently irretrievably. Some are even out of business. Despite the risks of ignoring TQM in today's highly competitive marketplace, some avoid it as a threat to their power and their comfort levels. So this group looked for a way to move ahead without the top level leadership usually required.

How did these middle managers and professional employees persuade their superiors to adopt TQM? They didn't persuade their superiors right away. Instead, they sneaked; they implemented TQM without more than the axiom "We told 'em, and silence is consent." Within their own plant, they began to practice total quality management, and began in their own work sections.

This approach is contrary to our previous advice about commitment and executive leadership in total quality. If you really want TQM, though, and can't get the support you need, it may be all that is possible. These individuals faced such a situation and decided to go ahead. If they had not succeeded in their first efforts, it is possible that all could have been lost, including their jobs, or at least some career time.

But they did succeed, and ultimately persuaded the whole subsidiary to adopt TQM. It appears likely that the corporate chief executive will take the leadership role and make TQM the whole company's way of doing business.

If you want to give your company the benefits of TQM, can you do what they did? You can, if your chief executive is merely reluctant or preoccupied, and not constitutionally incapable of leading such an effort. If your CEO can be persuaded eventually, you may be able to do what these managers and workers did. The steps of introducing TQM are the same, changing only what must be changed in the circumstances.

For chief executive commitment and leadership, the plant management must be substituted. It may be necessary to undertake study outside working hours. Training may have to be accomplished internally, since a budget for retaining outside consultants may be unattainable. The guerilla TQM effort we are describing began by training a few to become experts. These experts them trained others in TQM practices. In such an approach, those selected to become experts must be carefully chosen, since they may not have the daily resource of an experienced consultant to draw on.

Good quality training is offered locally in many parts of North America by the American Production and Control Society (APICS) and by the American Society for Quality Control (ASQC). For accountants specifically, the Institute of Management Accountants (IMA) offers some good material and has begun a new Continuous Improvement Center at its headquarters in Montvale, New Jersey. (For more information, call 800-638-4427.) These organizations are also good sources of contacts who can offer their suggestions and telephone assistance, both in concrete experiences and psychological support. Such organizations are also a good resource since companies will often support memberships and training even when not officially committed to an overall TQM implementation.

Despite all the support that can be brought to bear locally, the lack of top-level sponsorship makes it harder. Reluctant workers must be carefully persuaded in cases where corporate sponsorship would have allowed them to be told "fake it 'til you make it." If TQM practices conflict with corporate policy or standard practices, compromises may be necessary, or the TQM practice may have to be forgone in some instances. But this is no excuse for neglecting to use those practices that can be implemented.

Success will usually persuade the unconvinced. Just as early successes in a fully supported, top-level-led implementation are sought to persuade doubters, early successes in a guerilla implementation can be used to get attention and persuade executive doubters. Continued successes in quality, cost, and delivery measures will eventually persuade even the most difficult bosses. In the case cited at the beginning of this section, it is spreading rapidly upward and has almost, but not yet quite, convinced the chief executive.

ROCKS AND SHOALS—AVOIDING COMMON PITFALLS

As we went through our discussions of TQM, we saw that there are a number of prerequisites in order for total quality to succeed, including strong leadership, a customer focus, clear goals, necessary data, and flexibility.

Neglect of any of these can lead to an ineffective total quality initiative, which dies out quickly when its corporate sponsor retires or takes another position. A typical complaint about American management is its short-term view of corporate results; each quarter is a new beginning. Both Asian and European managers take a longer-term view. The Germans even provide accounting reserves that act like savings accounts to transfer income among periods, smoothing out reported operating results. They feel that short time periods are too volatile to measure the economic performance of a company.

Commitment

TQM requires a long-term commitment to fundamental change. A sustained commitment is required, and until total quality becomes so much a part of an organization that its principles are employed naturally, without conscious attention, it must be driven into the organization by constant reiteration and example. Such an example must persist despite the fact that TQM will not solve all a company's problems or avert all calamities.

Many of the recent apparent TQM failures occurred because management "cut and ran" at the first sign of difficulty—not difficulty with TQM, but changes in competitive conditions or, for defense contractors particularly, changes in demand. Such externally caused factors can be anticipated by a total quality company as well as by anyone else, but probably no better. The same information is available to everyone in the market.

Sometimes, a TQM "sponsor" reaches retirement age, or is lured away to another company. If the effort depended too much on one individual, and is not yet well established, it can gradually (or quickly) die out.

Another source of problems in staying power is in the changes in product demand mentioned for the defense industry. When demand changes radically, and layoffs occur, it is hard for both management and the workforce to believe that there isn't some relationship. Rationally, we know there is none, but *post hoc, ergo propter hoc* is an unavoidable impression.

Just like any established habit, the habits of authoritarian, "hunch-based" management are hard to change. It takes constant watchfulness to avoid slipping back into old patterns. Only sustained, genuine commitment can bring about such a basic change in habits. It can be hard when other forces are pushing an organization, but it must be done to assure success.

Instant Pudding

Dr. Deming cautions against what he calls *instant pudding*. Results do not happen overnight. They follow training, acclimatization, and practice of new techniques and approaches to supervision and work. Too often, though, we look for results right away. "We announced TQM last month. Where are our inventory reductions, negligible warranty claims, and wonderful new work flows? Why is there still scrap and rework? Let's see the fine new accounting information that describes real events in the company and that does so immediately."

Remember that a good deal of work is required before the first permanent quality circle is formed. That will usually be the executive quality circle or quality steering committee, which operates at a level where action teams are few because the real work of producing what customers buy is done further down in the organization. The first few improvement proposals from working-level circles or teams will typically be some months into the TQM implementation.

While attention must be paid to the early successes as examples and encouragement to others, individual improvements will be minor. By itself, no one improvement will radically change the operations or profitability of the company. Over time, continuous improvement through TQM will transform the organization, but it will usually take several years. During this time, other factors will also affect the organization. It is possible to lose faith if outside forces impact the company negatively at the same time TQM is implemented. The proper question is not only "What has happened since we started on total quality?" but also "What would have happened if we hadn't started on total quality?"

Companies looking for quick, radical results will almost certainly be disappointed. It will take time to change attitudes and beliefs. It will take time for improvements to accumulate to affect the customer response, product quality, and profitability of the company significantly. Further, these things will occur gradually, a small step at a time. Each small improvement will slightly alter attitudes and results. Total quality will become part of the company a little at a time, and will become less and less distinct from normal operations. Eventually, it will be so much a part of the culture that it will not be noticed as a separate effort. But these changes will not occur instantly, or even quickly. There is no "instant pudding." Expecting it can damage or doom a TQM implementation.

Too Many Teams

Most of us have an action orientation. If we hear of a problem, the first thing we ask is, "What is being done about it?" If we think our superiors want something, we want to produce it right away. In the same way, if we think our superiors want total quality management, and we are among those who mentally "sign up," we will want to produce results.

Since TQM appears to consist of quality circles and action teams, one of our first responses is likely to be to begin a hunt for opportunities to form action teams and make improvements. This attitude is certainly natural and commendable. It must be tempered by wisdom, though.

At first we won't know how to find opportunities, how to evaluate them for potential impact, or what approaches are likely to work. While it is important to get started, it is also important to prepare. Remember that the opening steps include training and guidance from skilled facilitators. Each circle learns to function independently, but does not begin doing so right away.

In some cases, this natural enthusiasm has led to quickly forming quality circles and action teams without clear direction or charters. Some of them become coffee clubs, some become study groups (not so bad, but not action oriented), some get lost discussing the cafeteria or break schedules, and some have even been known to spend months deciding on names for themselves!

Remember that TQM is participative but also disciplined. Its purpose is to bring the skills, knowledge, and interests of the members of the organization to bear on customer satisfaction. Forming too many teams too soon outstrips the ability of the facilitators and trainers to imbue the specific TQM skills, knowledge, and approaches in the organizational components and individual associates of the company. Without orientation and training, coupled with orderly guidance in the early going, the willing enthusiasm of the associates can easily lose its focus. It can drift into discussions of impressions and opinions. Of the three attributes of TQM listed at the opening of the book, it remains participative, but loses its character as customer focused and data driven.

Further, we have observed that it is important in any new management effort that there be early successes to demonstrate the value of TQM and to encourage others. There will be some failures and disappointments among action teams eventually, but they should be avoided until the organization has accepted the workability of the total quality approach to management. Forming too many circles and teams too soon, before the necessary training and discipline are achieved and beyond the ability of the TQM implementation office to keep track and assist, will lead to undirected effort and premature examples of failure.

One easy trap is to try to move too fast and form too many teams before the organization is ready to use them effectively. It can be avoided by a planned, disciplined implementation with skilled, experienced guidance.

The Fair Labor Standards Act (FSLA) and Company Unions

In a well-publicized case, the National Labor Relations Board (NLRB) ruled that worker committees were within the prohibition of the National

Labor Relations Act of 1935. That act forbids an employer to "dominate or interfere with the formation or administration of any labor organization."

While it is unclear at this time how far this ruling goes, it is known that the worker committees or circles in the case discussed working conditions, but the company did not allow the workers to appoint their own representatives through free elections within an independent labor organization (union).

This trap can be avoided in a number of ways:

1. If a company is unionized, the union can be invited to participate in the TQM decision and its implementation from the beginning, with union members or representatives at every level.

2. Quality circles and action teams should confine their activities to work methods and product issues. They should not discuss working conditions and terms of employment, in general. A circle or team whose work actually was a part of working conditions or terms of employment, such as cafeteria workers, plant engineering, or personnel departments, might be an exception.

3. Management cannot take back what it has given. Too often, managers want the good feeling of acting participative, but as soon as the going gets hard, their underlying distrust of workers comes out. If you're going to have the workforce as a partner with management, you must do so genuinely. Employees will act like partners only if they are partners.

At this writing, it isn't clear how this decision will affect TQM implementation in other companies. The suggestions given above are no insurance that trouble can be averted. They do, however, attempt to address the concerns of the NLRB and of existing employee organizations such as unions, while reducing the chance that insincerity will eventually lead to an unhappy worker bringing a complaint.

CONCLUSION

Total quality management is not a magic "cure for what ails ya." It requires changes in attitude and in relationships that have been developed over many years. In making such thoroughgoing changes, it is possible to take wrong turns, to miss some helpful or essential components, or to slide unknowingly into a trap.

Some of these potential difficulties can be recognized, anticipated, and avoided. Among these are lack of commitment and staying power, expecting quick transformation, forming too many teams before they are ready to work effectively, and inadvertently getting into "company union" situations. These potential problems need not occur if they are consciously dealt with in both planning stages and execution.

INDEX